Russ Alan Prince

David A. Geracioti

CULTIVATING THE MIDDLE-CLASS MILLIONAIRE

WHY FINANCIAL ADVISORS ARE FAILING
THEIR WEALTHY CLIENTS
AND WHAT THEY CAN DO ABOUT IT

Cultivating the Middle-Class Millionaire
Why Financial Advisors Are Failing Their Wealthy Clients
and What They Can Do About It
Insights, Methodologies, Tools and Tactics

by Russ Alan Prince with David A. Geracioti

WEALTH MANAGEMENT PRESS

9800 Metcalf Avenue
Overland Park, KS 66212

ISBN number 0-89287-987-4

To Jerry,
Yesterday, Today & Forever
Russ Alan Prince

CULTIVATING THE MIDDLE-CLASS MILLIONAIRE

WHY FINANCIAL ADVISORS ARE FAILING THEIR WEALTHY CLIENTS AND WHAT THEY CAN DO ABOUT IT

Table of Contents

Foreword

CULTIVATING THE MIDDLE-CLASS MILLIONAIRE

Financial advisors continually ask us for tools to help them attract and retain clients and grow their practices. That is one of the reasons why we established Wealth Management Press, the imprint of *Registered Rep.* and *Trusts & Estates* magazines. Now, I'm pleased to present *Cultivating the Middle-Class Millionaire*, the results of an extensive survey of the perceptions of high-net-worth investors and their financial advisors—and more important-ly, the best source of material that will enable financial advisors to grow their practices by successfully finding and working with the affluent.

Cultivating the Middle-Class Millionaire is based on the most up-to-date re-search of financial advisors ideal clients: investors with between $500,000 and $5 million of liquid assets. The purpose of this book is to provide fi-nancial advisors with an understanding of middle-class millionaires' world and to introduce advisors to the process that creates loyal clients. After all, middle-class millionaires are the clients who readily give you more money, act as Apostles for your practice and enable you to be a true wealth manager. If it all clicks for you, you may be able to increase your income by a third or more within the first year, and you will have the systems in place to win new middle-class millionaires from your current clients, as well as accountants and attorneys who advise this group.

To make this book happen, we teamed up with *The New Yorker* to study more than 1,400 middle-class millionaires. We also researched more than 500 financial advisors for comparative purposes. We turned to Russ Alan Prince, the leading authority on private wealth, and *Registered Rep.* Editor-in-Chief David A. Geracioti, to craft this book.

I personally thank Russ, David and the readers and staff of *The New Yorker* for making this possible.

Warren N. Bimblick
Publisher
Wealth Management Press
New York, New York

September 15, 2005

HOW TO USE THIS BOOK

It is a grim reality: Most financial advisors want affluent clients. In fact, in the studies we have performed over 16 years, finding and winning wealthy clients is without question the financial advisor's number one concern. That's what makes the reality so grim: the competition is brutal. Every advisor—from the registered independent investment advisor working out of his house to the Merrill Lynch rep at a suburban branch—wants to land wealthy clients. The purpose of this book is to give you an edge in doing just that. The best way to land high-net-worth (HNW) clients is to understand what their financial needs are, what they are worried about and how they view their jobs, their businesses and their money and investments. More important, we offer strategies for helping you win the wealthy clients that every firm and financial advisor has been talking about.

The good news is that there is ample opportunity to exploit the high-net-worth market. One major finding in researching this book: Many HNW advisors don't understand their clients, and are, therefore, not providing adequate professional services. Indeed, we've found a gap in how advisors view themselves and how their HNW clients truly view them. In short, advisors tend to think their HNW clients are interested in what they, the financial advisors, consider themselves to be good at. And that's what makes up the guts of this book.

We surveyed by phone 1,417 wealthy retail clients—defined as having $500,000 to $5 millions in liquid assets. To get a reliable and representative sample, we polled a database of wealthy readers of *The New Yorker* magazine. We asked our affluent respondents a wide range of questions on financial issues, everything from their biggest financial concerns to their interest in various financial vehicles, such as hedge funds.

The research's findings helped us create clear guidelines on how financial advisors can build a profitable practice by finding and helping these affluent clients. From the thousand-odd conversations, we discovered a financial advisory practice framework that, when applied systematically, results in tremendous client loyalty. And, as you undoubtedly have learned, the financial benefits of client loyalty can be exceptional. Just as important we also define the concept of wealth management. Everyone talks about it, but, truth be told, too many advisors don't know what it means. We also offer strategies for finding new middle-class millionaire clients.

In addition, by using a database provided by Primedia Business Information, publishers of *Registered Rep.* magazine, the leading magazine for financial professionals, we also surveyed 512 financial advisors for their attitudes and perceptions about their wealthy clients. When you compare the results of the two—how HNW clients view their advisors and how advisors think their clients view them—you find some enormous gaps. Indeed, advisors have no clue about how their HNW clients regard them. We found that most financial advisors are advisor-centric as opposed to client-centric, in spite of proclamations to the contrary. We learned from our research that advisors tend to think their clients are interested in the things that the advisors themselves are interested in, such as learning about mutual funds, for example. (Across the board, HNW clients cared less about learning more about mutual funds, but instead thirsted for knowledge about hedge funds.) Not surprisingly, greater success is in store for client-centric financial advisors. Finally, we have incorporated the findings from other empirical studies we have conducted in an effort to provide additional insights and perspectives about the needs of the HNW investor.

While the data are interesting and useful, the real import of this book is the advice offered on how to win more HNW business. There are any number of methods, tactics and tools that you can use to become significantly more successful with these wealthy individuals. The research shows you what needs to be done; the strategies show you how to do it.

In coaching financial advisors to reach elite status (defined as grossing $1 million or more for more than two years in a row), we have found that providing research findings and even practical advice is sometimes not enough. Sometimes a financial advisor has to "think different" (as Apple Computer used to put it). This book will help you think about your practice in a more analytical way so that you'll be able to more creatively tweak your business plan.

Take a moment to answer the following questions.

The Rich

Which "rich people" are not "rich?"
What are the most pressing concerns of the affluent?
What products and services are of interest to the wealthy?
What does a loyal client do for your practice?
Are your clients loyal?
How do you instill loyalty in your affluent clients?

Your Practice

Are you a wealth manager? What does being a wealth manager mean anyway? How is that different from the average financial advisory practice? If you are a wealth manager, what happened to your income since you have made the transition from an "average" financial advisor?

Your Clients

How well do you understand your most important affluent clients? How much do you really know about them? It might sound silly, but do these clients have pets? If they have pets, what are the pets' names? Financial advisors who knew more about their HNW clients, including the names of their pets, were likely to have more than twice the assets under management as those who did not, our surveys found.

How good are you at meeting prospective affluent clients? Of the prospective clients you meet, how effective are you at winning new business? What is the best way to source new affluent clients?

Examine Yourself

One goal of this book is to get you thinking. If you want to build a successful financial advisory practice catering to the so-called middle-class millionaire (the subject of the next chapter), you will see there is no simple strategy for meeting and closing rich clients—conference speakers' assertions notwithstanding. (After nearly 20 years in the business, we have seen all manner of snake oil salesman at conferences presenting "magic bullet" schemes for landing rich clients; very few, it seems to us, really have the facts to back up their assertions.)

In coaching financial advisors, we find that getting them to think critically about their practices can be especially difficult. As coaches, it is our goal to help advisors "think different," but also to achieve meaningful changes in their practices that would translate into, at a minimum, a 25 percent increase in income in the first year. We will be drawing from our experience coaching financial advisors throughout the book in order to make the material more practical for you; it will also help understand the issues better. (For information on choosing a coach see *The Appendix: The Seven Guidelines for Selecting a Coach*).

In order to become proficient at the process of cultivating and working with whom we call "middle class" millionaires (more on why we call them middle-class millionaires later), you will need to examine your practice objectively.

- You will need to describe and quantify what you are doing today.
- You will need to define what you want to accomplish and establish an appropriate business model.
- You will need to establish a protocol for creating loyal clients.
- You will have to create a strategy for sourcing new wealthy clients.

We will provide you with empirically derived insights, field-proven strategies, but you will have to examine the issues thoughtfully, and then customize them to your own personality, working style and goals. To get the most from this book, you will also need to:

- *Become comfortable with the research findings.* This entails studying the results and how to apply them. Remember, we are looking at the wealthy in the aggregate. On a one-to-one basis, obviously each wealthy person's financial needs are unique. Nevertheless, the research does indeed provide meaningful insights that are useful in working with the HNW (and all kinds of other retail investors, for that matter).

- *Be honest with yourself.* Every financial advisor we know says he is client-centered. Yet we have solid empirical evidence that most are not. Don't be afraid to take the research results and ask tough questions about your own client relationships. For instance, we have found that most financial advisors say they have all the investable assets of their top affluent clients. However, when we query affluent clients, they tell us they tend to employ a number of financial advisors, carving up assets among them.

- *Incorporate the methodologies, tools and tactics into your practice.* It is important to understand the data, but do not to get too bogged down and overly analytical. The research findings only point the way. Success can be won by capitalizing on the research with field-proven strategies.

To help absorb the data and the resulting strategies, there are questions and exercises at the end of each chapter. The exercises will help you understand the data and will enable you to better customize the methodologies, tools and tactics to your unique situation. They will help you understand what it takes to cultivate "middle class" millionaires, the subject of the next chapter.

If you actually think about the questions in each chapter and then complete the exercises, you will be able to evaluate your own practice. And then you will be in a position to adopt the appropriate strategies to attain your financial advisory practice goals. That's how you will get the most from this book.

PART
1

THE
MIDDLE-CLASS
MILLIONAIRE

Millionaire But Still Middle-Class?

- *How much money and assets does it take to make a person wealthy?*
- *Which "rich people" are not "rich?"*
- *Can you describe your "ideal client?"*
- *What are some of the core characteristics of your "ideal client?"*

In the 1920s in a Parisian café, so the story goes, the writer F. Scott Fitzgerald begins to try to tell Ernest Hemingway that the rich are different from the non-rich. "Yeah," Hemingway answers sarcastically, "they have more money." Actually, Hemingway was more correct than he could have known, at least that's what our data show. We found that, in aggregate, wealthy people don't consider themselves wealthy. Well, they consider themselves wealthy, but not in the way you would think. They fear losing their jobs or businesses and about leaving something for their heirs. And they, like the rest of us, worry about wasting money and getting value for the things that they buy. That said, as you'll see, the fabulously wealthy are in fact different, in the Fitzgerald meaning.

To most of the world, people with $500,000 in liquid assets are wealthy, no doubt about it (to say nothing of those who have millions in liquid assets). Yet, interestingly, we found that the high-net-worth (HNW) we polled wouldn't define themselves as rich. In fact, what we discovered is that virtually all respondents regard themselves as middle class. Some would say they are upper-middle class, but they strongly tend to identify themselves as being middle class. To them, the rich are people with expensive yachts and a garage full of exotic sports cars.

In our national phone survey of 1,417 millionaires, we found that 42.6 percent of them see themselves as middle class and the remaining 57.4 percent see themselves as upper-middle class (Exhibit 1.1). Moreover, we found that they—in total—do not see themselves as wealthy.

Exhibit 1.1 | Social Position of the Wealthy

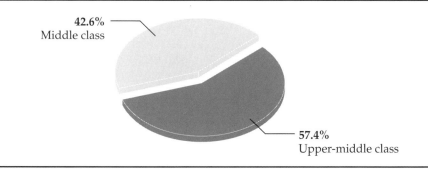

42.6%
Middle class

57.4%
Upper-middle class

N = 1,417 Middle-Class Millionaires

Wealthy, to many of our respondents, is someone else. Again, a wealthy person might own a 120-foot yacht. A wealthy person might have an art collection full of Picassos and Rembrandts. A wealthy person can walk into a watch store and walk out with a top-of-the-line Patek Philippe. Those are rich people. "Middle-class" millionaires do not feel comfortable buying such luxurious goods casually and, therefore, are not "rich."

Based on their strongly held position that they are middle class, we refer to this segment of the affluent as middle-class millionaires. Their values, their concerns, their actions place them squarely in the middle class. Their actual wealth, then, doesn't make them "rich" in their own minds; and they don't think about their wealth in comparison to the wealth of others.

While middle-class millionaires are indeed wealthier than true middle-class people, they tend to confront many of the same issues—paying for college, covering the mortgage every month, socking away retirement money, you name it. For middle-class millionaires, the only difference tends to be in degree. But their lifestyles are nicer than the true middle-class cohort, and, therefore, are more expensive to maintain. Most of them, despite their assets, must continue to earn—and they have all the stress and anxieties that go along with a high-earning career. They can't be rich, the middle-class millionaire says: The rich do not need to work and are not beset by the stress of having to, say, pay the mortgage every month.

Let's now take a closer look at our sample of middle-class millionaires.

Sample Demographics

In our survey, 53.9 percent of the people have a net-worth between $1 million and $3 million (Exhibit 1.2). The rest (46.1 percent) have a net-worth between $3 million and $10 million.

Exhibit 1.2 | Net-worth Segments

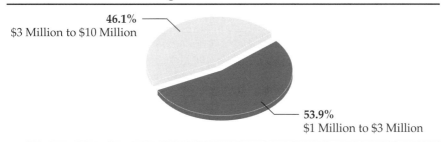

46.1%
$3 Million to $10 Million

53.9%
$1 Million to $3 Million

N = 1,417 Middle-Class Millionaires

In liquid assets, 34.1 percent have between $500,000 and $1 million (Exhibit 1.3). Nearly half (46.5 percent) have investable assets between $1 million and $2 million. The remainder (19.4 percent) has between $2 million and $6 million.

Exhibit 1.3 | Investable Asset Segments

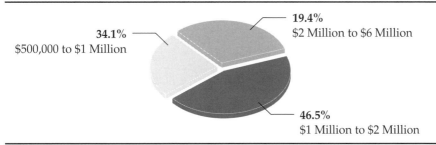

19.4%
$2 Million to $6 Million

34.1%
$500,000 to $1 Million

46.5%
$1 Million to $2 Million

N = 1,417 Middle-Class Millionaires

The majority of middle-class millionaires (44.5 percent) are between 55 and 65 years old (Exhibit 1.4). Almost a third (31 percent) are under 55 years old and about a quarter of them (24.5 percent) are 65 years old or older.

Exhibit 1.4 | Age

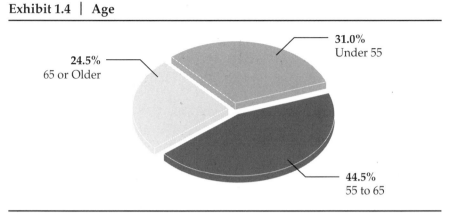

24.5%
65 or Older

31.0%
Under 55

44.5%
55 to 65

N = 1,417 Middle-Class Millionaires

Most are male (67.8 percent) which, considering all our previous research, is not surprising (Exhibit 1.5). While women are increasingly becoming wealthy, they still have not closed the gap with men when it comes to being millionaires.

Exhibit 1.5 | Gender

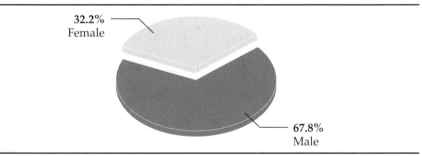

32.2%
Female

67.8%
Male

N = 1,417 Middle-Class Millionaires

How do people become middle-class millionaires? (See Exhibit 1.6). The majority (44.9 percent) became affluent by working hard, climbing the corporate ladder and being well compensated for their efforts. Included here are those who wisely invested a portion of their incomes. Often a sizable portion of their liquid assets is in their company's stock.

About one in five (21.3 percent) own their own company and are wealthy because of it. In general, these affluent business owners are likely to have most of their net-worth tied up in their companies. This cohort is less likely to be as liquid as the other middle-class millionaires we surveyed.

Retirement account rollovers were the primary source of wealth for 16.4 percent of the middle-class millionaires. These affluent individuals are older and the assets are most always liquid.

Less than one in ten (9.4 percent) inherited their wealth. And fewer still (8 percent) became affluent from the sale of a company. Most of their wealth is liquid.

Exhibit 1.6 | Source of Wealth

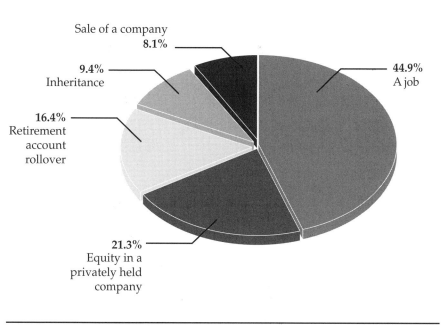

Sale of a company
8.1%

9.4%
Inheritance

16.4%
Retirement
account
rollover

44.9%
A job

21.3%
Equity in a
privately held
company

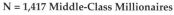

N = 1,417 Middle-Class Millionaires

Net Worth Determines Perceived Status

When do peope view themselves as upper-middle class? Only one factor makes a meaningful difference. The amount of liquid assets doesn't matter, nor does a person's age or gender. Nor does the source of the wealth make a difference. What makes a difference is net worth (Exhibit 1.7). Three quarters of the respondents with between $3 million and $10 million (75.3 percent) identified themselves as upper-middle class. Meanwhile, 41.5 percent of respondents with between $1 million and $3 million identified themselves as upper-middle class.

Exhibit 1.7 | Social Position by Net Worth

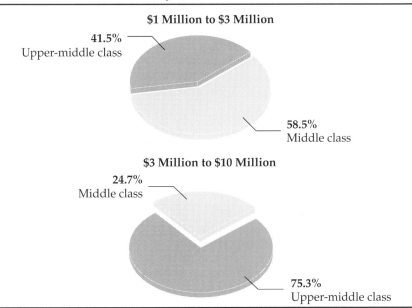

N = 1,417 Middle-Class Millionaires

What this tells us is that the affluent use their total financial position in conceptualizing their social status. While the amount of liquid assets a client has is a dominant measure used by much of the financial services industry, it is not how the wealthy think about their wealth. Therefore, you should be aware of—if not strongly focused on identifying and understanding—the net worth of your clients and their prospects, even if your financial advisory practice is exclusively about *managing investments*.

Middle-Class Millionaires Are the "Ideal Client"

It seems a little strange to say that middle-class millionaires are an under-served or poorly served market in the United States. In *Chapter 4: The Value of Loyalty*, we see that only 13.8 percent of middle-class millionaires can be identified as loyal to their financial advisors. This is a very low percentage, especially considering that for most financial advisors, as well as financial institutions, middle-class millionaires are "ideal clients."

In our study, we asked financial advisors to rate a number of factors that we then used to construct their "ideal clients." A few of the determining factors were:

- Preferred age of the client

- Investable assets
- Financial issues and challenges they face
- Cost-structure for the delivery of financial products and services
- Competitive pressures

Based on statistical analyses, we were able to conclude that 86.1 percent of the financial advisors are looking at middle-class millionaires as their "ideal clients" (Exhibit 1.8). The remaining 13.9 percent of financial advisors were defining their "ideal client" as having substantially more wealth. And, even in this cohort, middle-class millionaires would rarely be turned away.

Exhibit 1.8 | Middle-class millionaires Are the "Ideal Client"

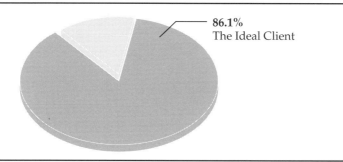

86.1%
The Ideal Client

N = 512 Financial Advisors

While everyone wants to work with wealthy clients, who have significant liquid assets, a key factor in the determination of the "ideal client" are the financial issues and challenges they face. Obviously, a financial advisor's ability to effectively handle complex financial situations enables him or her to move upscale. For the majority of financial advisors, managing complex client situations is a stumbling block to dealing with wealthier and more successful clients. However, by adopting a team approach, this stumbling block can be overcome (see *Chapter 10: Your Wealth Management Team*).

It is not only the financial advisors who are focusing in on middle-class millionaires, senior management at brokerage firms, independent broker/ dealers and private banks also consider middle-class millionaires to be the high-net-worth "sweet spot." In fact, using a similar statistical approach, we found that 83.6 percent of the senior executives from these financial institutions identified the middle-class millionaire as their firm's "ideal client" (Exhibit 1.9).

This was most pronounced among the brokerage firms (90.2 percent), somewhat less among the senior executives at independent broker/dealers (84.9 percent) and even proportionately less among the private banks (79.5

percent). Still, it is clear that the greater majority of senior executives at financial institutions are seeking to target middle-class millionaires.

Exhibit 1.9 | Middle-Class Millionaires Are the "Sweet Spot" for Financial Institutions

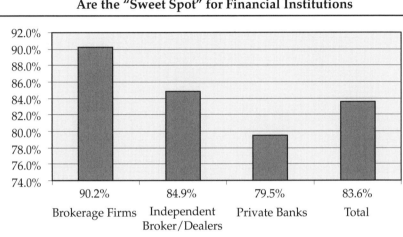

Brokerage Firms	Independent Broker/Dealers	Private Banks	Total
90.2%	84.9%	79.5%	83.6%

N = 269 Senior Executives at Financial Institutions

Without question, we have found few financial advisors who are not interested in working with HNW clients. Across the spectrum of financial advisors, as well as financial institutions, middle-class millionaires can be considered the "sweet spot" in the financial services industry. These are the affluent that are within reach and for whom most financial advisors can be of meaningful assistance. Moreover, these are the type of clients who can enable financial advisors to have highly successful practices.

What is also important to realize is that the methodologies, tools and tactics we detail throughout the book can be applied to wealthier clients. The Whole Client Model, for instance, is critical in providing wealth management services to middle-class millionaires and it is equally critical for offering similar expertise to family offices and ultra high-net-worth clients. (See *Chapter 9: The Whole Client Model.*) Furthermore, the optimal methodology for sourcing new middle-class millionaires is conceptually the same and even more central for sourcing wealthier clients. (See *Chapter 13: Creating a Pipeline of New Middle-Class Millionaire Clients from Accountants and Attorneys.*) In conclusion, by mastering what it takes to cultivate middle-class millionaires, you are in an excellent position to move up-market and cultivate even wealthier clients. (See *Afterwords: Moving Up-Market.*)

Practice Implications

For financial advisors it is important to recognize that what—by most standards—is a lot of money does not necessarily mean a person perceives himself as wealthy. When it takes more and more money to make the Forbes 400 list, having a net worth of a "mere" $7 million can readily "put one in one's place"—and that place is not always among the "rich."

Again, middle-class millionaires do not see themselves as being rich. Of course, by most definitions, they are. And their affluence—whether in the form of liquid or illiquid assets—makes them prime candidates for financial advice and a broad range of products. They are the "ideal client" for most financial advisors, as well as the various financial institutions.

That said net worth is the principal factor in how millionaires define their social status. We have found that a great many financial advisors who provide investment management expertise fail to familiarize themselves with the net worth of their clients.

———————

Take a few moments and think about your current clients.
- *How many of your current clients are middle-class millionaires?*
- *How much are they worth?*
- *How much do they have in liquid assets?*
- *How many would categorize themselves as middle class?*
- *Or are they upper-middle class?*
- *Does anybody regard themselves as rich?*

———————

Exercise #1 | Net Worth and Your Book

1. Take a piece of paper and write down ten of your better middle-class millionaire clients.
2. For each client, specify his or her net worth.
3. Now, identify all the asset and liabilities for each of the ten middle-class millionaire clients.
4. After you broke out their assets and liabilities, how close was your estimate of their net worth?

We have found that, for the most part, financial advisors underestimate the net worth of their affluent clients. If you did the same, then there are probably considerably more untapped business opportunities available from your current clientele. Tapping these opportunities should be considered like low hanging fruit: an easy way for you to quickly provide a boost—usually a very large boost—to your income.

Exercise #2 | Your "Ideal Client"

1. Using the following criteria, define your "ideal client:"
   - Investable assets
   - Net worth
   - Financial issues and challenges he or she faces
   - Age and gender
   - Future business potential
     - More business from the client
     - Referrals to family and peers
   - Personal characteristics/rapport
   - Cost to acquire affluent clients
   - Ongoing costs of maintaining your relationship with affluent clients
2. Consider your ten best clients:
   - How many of them fit your "ideal client" profile?
   - How many are middle-class millionaires?
   - To what extent does the middle-class millionaire fit your "ideal client" profile?

If you are like most financial advisors, you have a solid number of middle-class millionaires as clients. And, naturally, you would like to have more. Also, we have found that most financial advisors who go through the exercise of constructing an "ideal client" profile find that the middle-class millionaire fits the profile very closely.

KEY CONCERNS OF MIDDLE-CLASS MILLIONAIRES

- *What is the biggest financial concern of middle-class millionaires?*
- *In general, how attuned are financial advisors to this concern?*
- *For example, which taxes do most middle-class millionaires abhor the most?*

Middle-class millionaires confront issues everyday just like everyone else. They would disabuse you of the notion that they lead a charmed life. On the contrary, while none are looking to give up their wealth, they are dealing with many of the same issues as other people; it is often just a matter of degree, and that is why they consider themselves middle class—they are just like everybody else.

At the same time, affluence does carry some added complications. First, and foremost, middle-class millionaires are worried about losing their wealth. They are also concerned about paying taxes. While no one is looking to not pay his fair share, mitigating taxes is certainly preferable. This is why some HNW individuals seek financial advice.

Middle-class millionaires also confront a variety of more sophisticated financial concerns. These range from making sure their heirs are well taken care of to making charitable gifts.

Another set of concerns centers on their discretionary investment portfolio. Here the biggest issue is choosing a high-quality investment advisor.

Plagued by Financial Fragility

Fortunes are made, and fortunes are lost. A sharp downturn in a personal investment portfolio, for instance, could deal a body blow to the net worth of someone who is over-exposed to equities.

Nearly nine out of ten of the middle-class millionaires (88.6 percent) are very concerned about losing their wealth (Exhibit 2.1). Those who consider themselves upper-middle class are more concerned than those who only see themselves as middle class—no doubt, because they have more at stake (92.7 percent compared to 82.9 percent).

Exhibit 2.1 | Very Concerned About Losing Their Wealth
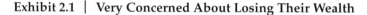

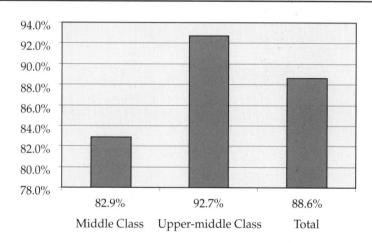

N = 1,417 Middle-Class Millionaires

Aside from not being particularly interested in downsizing their lifestyles, we found that many middle-class millionaires are engaging in a financial balancing act. Truth be told, they are often only a few steps away from significant financial reversals. Consequently, they tend to worry about making sure they maintain their lifestyles. And that can only be done by maintaining, protecting—and in some cases, even growing—their wealth.

As we noted, we also surveyed 512 financial advisors about their perceptions of their middle-class millionaire clients which, for this course of research we defined as clients having between $500,000 to $5 million in investable assets. Private bankers represented 15.4 percent of the respondents, registered representatives 54.9 percent and independent financial advisors 29.7 percent.

The Disconnect

The disconnect between advisors and their clients begins here: Only 15.4 percent of the financial advisors believed 20 percent or more of their clients with these levels of investable assets are very concerned about losing their wealth. This perception is in dramatic contrast to what middle-class millionaires told us (Exhibit 2.2). While you might be much more in-synch with your middle-class millionaire clients than most financial advisors, what is clear in this example (and we will see it repeated again and again) is that most financial advisors don't really understand their affluent clients. An in-depth understanding of affluent clients is absolutely critical in order for the overwhelming majority of financial advisors to be successful.

Exhibit 2.2 | Perception of Financial Advisors

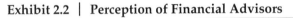

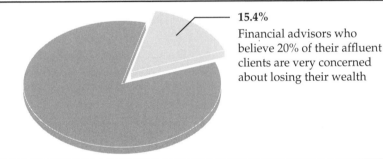

15.4%
Financial advisors who believe 20% of their affluent clients are very concerned about losing their wealth

N = 512 Financial Advisors

There are many tools that are employed by financial advisors to help them understand their clients. In coaching elite financial advisors (consistent annual incomes of $1 million or more), we are privileged to be able to see what works best in the trenches. By collecting and systematizing the fact-finding methodologies of these elite advisors, we have been able to derive a holistic system for gathering affluent client data (see the "Whole Client Model," described in detail in Chapter 9).

While the Whole Client Model—which profiles the affluent client holistically—is the cornerstone of a prosperous wealth management practice, it is also necessary for financial advisors who focus exclusively on investment management (in other words, picking profitable investments, say, or picking out-performing asset managers). Unless an investment manager continually delivers stellar investment performance, then it is wise to create loyal clients who are willing to ride out the inevitable downturns. The Whole Client Model can be extremely helpful in this regard.

Aside from not losing their wealth, middle-class millionaires confront a wide variety of issues. We divided these issues into three categories:

- Taxes
- Personal interests and responsibilities
- Investment management

Taxes

Very few people want to pay taxes. The real issue is the extent to which they do not want to pay taxes, and which taxes are considered most egregious.

The majority of middle-class millionaires (84.7 percent) are most interested in mitigating income taxes (Exhibit 2.3). Income taxes have the most immediate and strongest impact on their day-to-day lives. The adverse consequences of these taxes are felt proportionately more by those with $1 million to $3 million (90.1 percent) than by their wealthier brethren (77.3 percent).

Not surprisingly, mitigating estate taxes is very important to 49.2 percent of middle-class millionaires. However, wealthier middle-class millionaires are disproportionately concerned than those with fewer assets (81.3 percent compared to 21.7 percent). Clearly, the more affluent are likely to be subject to estate taxes thereby prompting their concern.

The same pattern is seen for mitigating capital gains taxes. Overall, 41.7 percent of middle-class millionaires are very interested in mitigating them. However, we see that slightly more than twice as many of the wealthier individuals are concerned (58.5 percent compared to 27.1 percent). This is a function of the wealthier middle-class millionaires having more of their wealth locked up in long-term investments from their own businesses to company stock and real estate.

Exhibit 2.3 | Tax Mitigation by Net Worth

Taxes	$1M to $3M	$3M to $10M	Total
Mitigating income taxes	90.1%	77.3%	84.7%
Mitigating estate taxes	21.7%	81.3%	49.2%
Mitigating capital gains taxes	27.1%	58.5%	41.7%

N = 1,417 Middle-Class Millionaires

Financial Advisors Are from Mars . . .

As with the matter of financial fragility, financial advisors—on average—fail to really understand their affluent clients. What we see with respect to mitigating taxes (and what we will see repeated often) is that financial advisors tend to project onto their clients their concerns or, at the very least, what they think is important.

Based on our survey of 512 financial advisors, advisors say that their affluent clients are most concerned with mitigating income taxes (77.9 percent). (See Exhibit 2.4.) Nearly the same percentage of financial advisors believe their affluent clients are very concerned about mitigating capital gains taxes (71.5 percent), which does not match the responses from the middle-class millionaires. More telling is that only 8.2 percent of the financial advisors believe their wealthy clients are concerned with estate taxes. Once again we find a disconnect—and an opportunity.

Exhibit 2.4 | Tax Mitigation: Very Important to Clients With $500,000 to $5 Million in Investable Assets

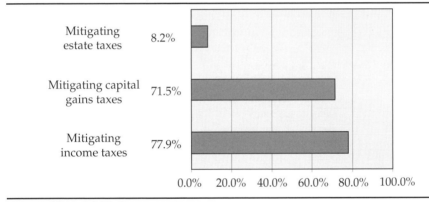

N = 512 Financial Advisors

Personal Interests and Responsibilities

Of course, middle-class millionaires are very concerned about a number of issues that we characterize as personal interests and responsibilities. As with the previous section, the net-worth of the middle-class millionaires often makes a difference. (See Exhibit 2.5.)

For nearly four out of five middle-class millionaires (79.2 percent), making sure their heirs are taken care of is a major concern. This is more the case for the wealthier middle-class millionaires as measured by net-worth (93.6 percent compared to 66.9 percent). This proves to be a tremendous opportunity for financial advisors as most middle-class millionaires have badly outdated estate plans. (See *Chapter 3: Financial Products and Services*.)

Having adequate medical insurance is important to 77.3 percent of the middle-class millionaires with insignificant differences among our net-worth segments.

Overall, 71.5 percent of our affluent sample is very concerned about having enough money in retirement. The less affluent are more concerned (87.3 percent compared to 53 percent). What is telling is that we find a significant difference based on net worth but no significant difference based on investable assets. For financial advisors working with middle-class millionaires on retirement distribution planning, it is essential to take into account their net worth and their lifestyle costs. We have found that relatively few financial advisors are engaging in retirement distribution planning based on a client's net worth.

About half the middle-class millionaires (48.3 percent) are concerned about paying for a child or grandchild's education. The less affluent are more concerned (65.2 percent compared to 28.6 percent) because they are financially less able to shoulder the cost.

Being sued is a big issue to about half (47.3 percent) of the middle-class millionaires. For the wealthier, it is more of an issue (58.8 percent compared to 37.4 percent). After all, the more affluent a person is the more they have to lose—and the more other people see them as meal tickets in the litigation lottery. Here we have another big opportunity because so few middle-class millionaires have taken steps to protect their assets from frivolous lawsuits. (See *Chapter 3: Financial Products and Services.*)

For two-fifths (40 percent) the prospect of losing their job or business creates high anxiety. About half the less wealthy (48.4 percent)—and nearly a third (30.5 percent) of the more affluent—feel this way. The wealthier middle-class millionaires have more of a cushion, but still tend to be living "on the edge."

For about a quarter (28.1 percent), there is serious concern over issues of personal security. This is the world of high-end home surveillance systems, personal protection specialists and crisis intervention plans. Logically, proportionately more of the wealthier middle-class millionaires are concerned (40.4 percent compared to 17.8 percent) as they have more at risk and are more likely to be targeted.

A similar number of middle-class millionaires (28.1 percent) are very concerned about taking care of their parents. This is more the case for those with $1 million to $3 million (38.4 percent) compared to those who are more affluent (16.1 percent). Once again, we see the financial cushion of greater total wealth coming into play.

Lastly, 27.8 percent of middle-class millionaires are very concerned with making meaningful gifts to charity. The wealthier ones are more concerned (34.8 percent compared to 21.9 percent).

When we turn our attention to the perceptions of financial advisors, we see that save for having adequate medical insurance (79.8 percent), many advisors tend not to recognize the concerns of their middle-class millionaire clients (Exhibit 2.6). Once again, we find a disconnect between middle-class millionaires and financial advisors who cater to them.

Exhibit 2.5 | Personal Interests and Responsibilities by Net Worth

Interests and Responsibilities	$1M to $3M	$3M to $10M	Total
Making sure your heirs are taken care of	66.9%	93.6%	79.2%
Having adequate medical insurance	78.1%	76.4%	77.3%
Having enough money in retirement	87.3%	53.0%	71.5%
Paying for children's or grandchildren's education	65.2%	28.6%	48.3%
Being sued	37.4%	58.8%	47.3%
Losing your job or business	48.4%	30.5%	40.0%
Having high quality personal security	17.8%	40.4%	28.2%
Taking care of parents	38.4%	16.1%	28.1%
Making meaningful gifts to charity	21.9%	34.8%	27.8%

N = 1,417 Middle-Class Millionaires

Exhibit 2.6 | Interests and Responsibilities—Very Important to Clients With $500,000 to $5 Million in Investable Assets

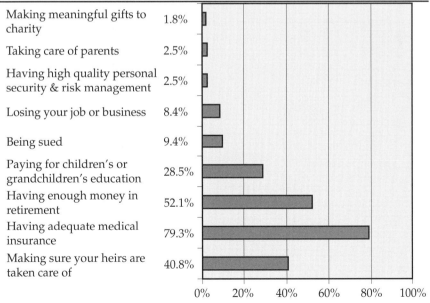

Making meaningful gifts to charity	1.8%
Taking care of parents	2.5%
Having high quality personal security & risk management	2.5%
Losing your job or business	8.4%
Being sued	9.4%
Paying for children's or grandchildren's education	28.5%
Having enough money in retirement	52.1%
Having adequate medical insurance	79.3%
Making sure your heirs are taken care of	40.8%

N = 512 Financial Advisors

Investment Management

When it comes to investment management, 72.7 percent of middle-class millionaires said that working with a high-quality investment advisor was a major concern (Exhibit 2.7). This was true for all surveyed, no matter how much they had in investable assets.

We also found that 11.9 percent of middle-class millionaires were concerned about diversifying their investment portfolios. For the less wealthy, the greater the concern was for diversification: 18.2 percent investors with discretionary portfolios of $500,00 to $1 million were concerned about diversifying portfolios, 11.2 percent for those with discretionary portfolios of $1 million to $2 million and just to 2.5 percent for those with $2 million to $6 million.

Exhibit 2.7 | Investment Management Concerns

Concerns	$500K to $1M	$1M to $2M	$2M to $6M	Total
Working with a high-quality investment advisor	70.4%	73.7%	74.2%	72.7%
Diversifying investment portfolios	18.2%	11.2%	2.5%	11.9%

N = 1,417 Middle-Class Millionaires

Again, when it comes to investment management, we find that financial advisors tend not to be on the same wavelength as their middle-class millionaire clients (Exhibit 2.8). Relatively speaking, more of the financial advisors place emphasis on the desire of these affluent investors to work with a high-quality investment advisor (83.2 percent) and to diversify their portfolios (33.4 percent).

Exhibit 2.8 | Interests and Responsibilities—Very Important to Clients With $500,000 to $5 Million in Investable Assets

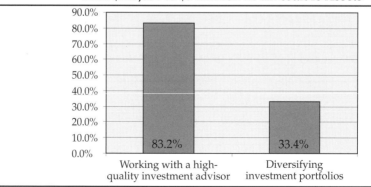

N = 512 Financial Advisors

No one does not want to work with a high-quality professional, obviously. What we are seeing is a matter of emphasis. Comparatively fewer middle-class millionaires are focusing as strongly on the investment aspect as the investment advisors themselves.

Practice Implications

What we are seeing is that financial advisors tend to view the world of the wealthy through their own biased perception of the financial world. In the aggregate, it is painfully clear that financial advisors have a warped and faulty understanding of what is truly important to their middle-class millionaire clients—and for the greater majority of advisors, their "ideal clients."

To be optimally successful in cultivating middle-class millionaires, it is imperative that you understand them. We are not talking about a superficial understanding, but a deep comprehension of each HNW client's financial needs. The research findings we discussed in this chapter provide broad insights. While these insights are effective in supplying general direction, in the final analysis you will need to develop an in-depth understanding of each and every one of your middle-class millionaire clients.

In thinking about your current clients:

- *How many are living close to the "edge?"*
- *How many are plagued by financial fragility?*
- *What is their viewpoint on your role as their financial advisor?*
- *How do you compare in importance to their other advisors?*

Exercise #1 | The Impact of Taxes

1. Write down your ten very best middle-class millionaire clients.
2. What is the impact of each of the three types of taxes—income, estate and capital gains—on their net worth? On their lifestyles?
3. Which of these three types of taxes is the biggest concern to each of these ten affluent clients?

Each of your affluent clients might very well be focused on different taxes because of his unique situation. We found that many financial advisors fail to be aware of the tax concerns of their clients—including their best clients—and are therefore not in a position to be of value to these clients.

As noted, taxes are of critical importance to middle-class millionaires. It is very important that you understand, in as much detail as possible, just how taxes affect your wealthy clients.

Exercise #2 | **Their Biggest Concerns**

1. Write down your ten very best middle-class millionaire clients.
2. For each of these middle-class millionaires identify their top three concerns.
3. Specify how you know these are their top concerns.
4. How are you helping them deal with each concern?

Much of the time, your job is not about managing assets. In fact, middle-class millionaires confront a wide variety of matters that are indirectly related to investing. You need to be very clear about their concerns and how your services can prove helpful. And, the answer is not always about investing performance.

FINANCIAL PRODUCTS AND SERVICES

- *Which financial products are middle-class millionaires interested in learning about?*
- *How many have estate plans?*
- *How many of those estate plans are "stale"?*

———————————————

Middle-class millionaires tend to own certain financial products and have availed themselves of a number of financial and legal services. But, they are interested in learning about other specific financial products and services.

Broadly speaking, you need to be aware of the basic products middle-class millionaires use—and, just as important, know the kinds of investment vehicles they are interested in. These insights will better enable you to introduce financial products and services that are more likely to get a positive response. According to our survey, financial advisors don't know what their HNW clients are interested in. This, too often, translates into financial advisors promoting the wrong financial product or service.

While these research-derived insights can be very powerful in helping you frame your approach to a middle-class millionaire, as we have repeatedly said, you need to be focused on the uniqueness of the individual (see *Chapter 9: The Whole Client Model*).

In this chapter we will look at the research findings concerning:

- Financial products
- Charitable giving
- Estate planning
- Asset protection planning

Financial Products

By taking the responses of the middle-class millionaires to a battery of questions concerning financial products, we were able to create a financial product grid (Exhibit 3.1). On the X-axis we have usage. This is the relative extent to which middle-class millionaires are using a financial product. For example, individual securities are the most widely used financial products. They are followed closely by mutual funds and life insurance.

On the Y-axis we have interest. This is a composite score describing the degree to which middle-class millionaires are interested in being exposed to or learning about a financial product. Returning to our previous examples, we find that middle-class millionaires are very interested in individual securities. On the other hand, they have little interest in either life insurance or mutual funds.

Exhibit 3.1 | Financial Product Grid

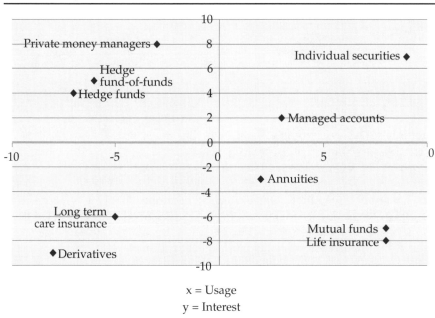

x = Usage

y = Interest

N = 1,417 Middle-Class Millionaires

Private money managers, hedge fund-of-funds and hedge funds—those products in the top left hand quadrant—are of acute interest to middle-class millionaires, and they have, to date, limited experience with them. You should, therefore, be able to discuss these financial products and be positioned to provide them if appropriate.

Individual securities and to a lesser degree managed accounts—top right hand quadrant—are familiar to middle-class millionaires. Moreover, they expect their financial advisors to be able to provide these products.

Long term care insurance and derivatives—bottom left hand quadrant—are not being used by middle-class millionaires because they are not interested in them. As products per se, they would be a very hard sell, but potentially necessary.

The products in the bottom right hand quadrant are being used by middle-class millionaires, some of them extensively. However, these affluent individuals are not very interested in someone pitching them annuities, life insurance or mutual funds.

This analysis is clearly financial product oriented. Without question, any particular middle-class millionaire will have needs and wants that can result in the purchase of a product that he or she is little interested in today. For example, very few people get excited at the prospect of purchasing life insurance. However, we have found that many middle-class millionaires, after going through the wealth management process, identify a need for life insurance and will (sometimes grudgingly) purchase the requisite amount and type. In these situations, the issue is not one of buying life insurance. Instead, the issue is solving a particular financial problem and life insurance is the preferred solution.

We have already seen that financial advisors tend not to understand their middle-class millionaire clients (see *Chapter 2: Key Concerns of Middle-Class Millionaires*). Moreover, we know that most middle-class millionaires would classify their financial advisors as advisor or product focused, which means they are more intent on "pitching" products than helping them deal with financial concerns and issues (see *Chapter 8: Wealth Management and the Middle-Class Millionaire*).

When we look at the findings of our survey of 512 financial advisors, we see that they tend to project their financial product preferences onto their middle-class millionaire clients (Exhibit 3.2). While the financial advisors were more on target with respect to individual securities and life insurance, they were way off target when it came to annuities and mutual funds.

**Exhibit 3.2 | Financial Products—Very Important to Clients with
$500,000 to $5 Million in Investable Assets**

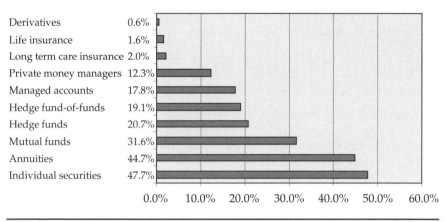

Derivatives	0.6%
Life insurance	1.6%
Long term care insurance	2.0%
Private money managers	12.3%
Managed accounts	17.8%
Hedge fund-of-funds	19.1%
Hedge funds	20.7%
Mutual funds	31.6%
Annuities	44.7%
Individual securities	47.7%

N = 512 Financial Advisors

It is important for you to be able to intelligently discuss all the relevant products with a wealthy client. Moreover, unless you want to tie your success exclusively to your client's investment performance, you will need to move beyond promoting products—the hot stock or the mutual fund of the month. You will need to become truly client-centric.

Charitable Giving

While only 27.8 percent of middle-class millionaires are concerned about making a meaningful gift to charity, 99.2 percent of them engage in "checkbook philanthropy" (Exhibit 3.3). This entails making checks to various nonprofits, mostly when the charity came calling. With so many of the middle-class millionaires involved with a charity, the next question is: Have they moved beyond current gifts to planned gifts?

Exhibit 3.3 | Engage in "Checkbook Philanthropy"

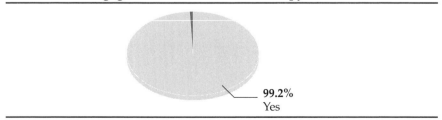

99.2%
Yes

N = 1,417 Middle-Class Millionaires

Only 21.1 percent of middle-class millionaires made a planned gift (Exhibit 3.4). A greater proportion of wealthier middle-class millionaires (30.8 percent) did so compared to the less wealthy (12.8 percent). Based on the findings, we can conclude that their greater wealth puts them in a position to make planned gifts. They are less likely to be concerned about needing the money in the future.

Exhibit 3.4 | Made One or More Planned Gifts

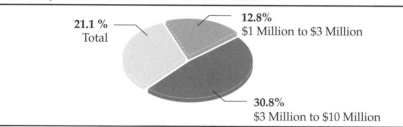

N = 1,417 Middle-Class Millionaires

When it comes to the type of planned gifts implemented by middle-class millionaires, donor advised funds win out (19.8 percent) (Exhibit 3.5). Charitable trusts were a somewhat distant second at 9.6 percent. Only 8.3 percent have made charitable will bequests. Then the percentages drop precipitously.

We do see a few differences among our net-worth segments. The wealthier middle-class millionaires are using donor advised funds, charitable trusts and private foundations. Meanwhile, the less affluent have gravitated to will bequests and charitable annuities.

Exhibit 3.5 | Types of Planned Gifts

Planned gift	$1M to $3M	$3M to $10M	Total
Donor advised funds	16.3%	21.4%	19.8%
Charitable trusts	1.0%	13.9%	9.6%
Will bequests	13.3%	6.0%	8.3%
Private foundations	0.0%	4.0%	2.8%
Charitable annuities	7.1%	0.0%	2.3%
Charitable gifts of life insurance	1.0%	2.5%	2.0%
Pooled income funds	2.0%	0.0%	0.6%
Supporting organizations	0.0%	0.5%	0.1%

N = 299 Middle-Class Millionaires

At the same time, 67.7 percent of middle-class millionaires are interested in learning more about private foundations (Exhibit 3.6). This is more evident among wealthier middle-class millionaires (78.6 percent compared to

58.4 percent). Next on the hierarchy are donor advised funds (40.0 percent), which are of more interest to the less affluent (49.9 percent compared to 28.5 percent). Half as many middle-class millionaires are interested in charitable trusts (19.1 percent); interest in various planned gifts decreases from there.

Exhibit 3.6 | Interested in Learning About Types of Planned Gifts

Planned gift	$1M to $3M	$3M to $10M	Total
Private foundations	58.4%	78.6%	67.7%
Donor advised funds	49.9%	28.5%	40.0%
Charitable trusts	15.3%	23.6%	19.1%
Charitable annuities	21.5%	4.9%	13.8%
Charitable gifts of life insurance	5.1%	1.2%	3.5%
Supporting organizations	0.8%	3.4%	2.0%
Pooled income funds	2.5%	0.3%	1.5%
Will bequests	0.0%	0.0%	0.0%

N = 1,417 Middle-Class Millionaires

In general, financial advisors do not accurately understand the interest middle-class millionaires have in various types of planned gifts (Exhibit 3.7). Whereas middle-class millionaires express no interest in will bequests, this type of planned gift is top of the list (45.5 percent) among financial advisors. Meanwhile, most financial advisors (14.5 percent) do not see their affluent clients being interested in private foundations; yet, the research with the affluent shows that they are indeed interested in private foundations.

Exhibit 3.7 | Planned Gifts—Interest in Learning About Them by Clients With $500,000 to $5 Million in Investable Assets

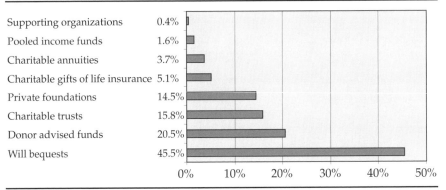

N = 512 Financial Advisors

All in all, when it comes to charitable planning and the various planned gifts, there are clearly opportunities for financial advisors to appropriately introduce various planned giving options to charitably inclined middle-class millionaires. However, financial advisors tend not to understand the possibilities. Again, by adopting a wealth management perspective, the appropriate opportunities with specific affluent clients will emerge.

Estate Planning

Another service that is appropriate for middle-class millionaires is estate planning. Recall that in *Chapter 2: Key Concerns of Middle-Class Millionaires* we noted that 79.2 percent are very concerned that their heirs are taken care of. Most middle-class millionaires (69.8 percent) have estate plans (Exhibit 3.8). However, as we will shortly see, this proves to be more of an opportunity to conduct or facilitate estate planning for these middle-class millionaires.

Exhibit 3.8 | Clients Who Have an Estate Plan

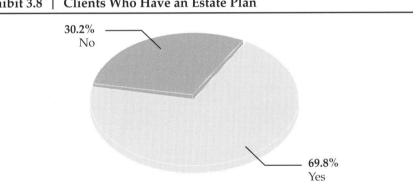

30.2%
No

69.8%
Yes

N = 1,417 Middle-Class Millionaires

The issue is when does an estate plan become "stale." To answer this question, we asked 101 private client lawyers (Exhibit 3.9). To be included in this study, each private client lawyer had to:
- Generate 51 percent or more of his or her billings by working with private clients as opposed to institutions, such as banks and charities.
- Provide planning services with a focus on estate planning.
- Have an average annual income over the previous 3 years of $400,000.

Nearly 10 percent see an estate plan as being stale within the year it is produced. Only 17.2 percent believe an estate plan has to be more than six years old before it is "stale." Another 21.6 percent consider an estate plan to be "stale" if it is one to two years old. At the same time, 52.3 percent consider an estate plan to be "stale" if it is between three and five years old.

Exhibit 3.9 | When an Estate Plan Is "Stale"

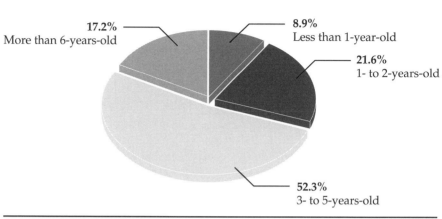

N = 101 Private Client Lawyers

Now, let's look at the age of the estate plan of our sample of middle-class millionaires (Exhibit 3.10). Nearly nine out of ten of the estate plans of middle-class millionaires (88.7 percent) are more than three years old. What is more telling is that the wealthier middle-class millionaires are likely to have "stale" estate plans because, as they became more affluent, they never updated their estate plans.

Exhibit 3.10 | Last Updated the Estate Plan

Last updated	$1M to $3M	$3M to $10M	Total
1 to 2 years ago	18.7%	2.5%	11.2%
3 to 5 years ago	42.5%	26.6%	35.1%
6 to 10 years ago	30.8%	45.8%	37.7%
11+ years ago	8.0%	25.1%	15.9%

N = 854 Middle-Class Millionaires

So the majority of middle-class millionaires either do not have an estate plan or it is stale, yet this situation is not recognized by the greater majority of financial advisors (Exhibit 3.11). Surprisingly, about four out of five (82.2 percent) financial advisors state that their affluent clients are all taken care of when it comes to estate planning. Again, this misperception, once corrected, opens the door for financial advisors to better serve these wealthy clients—as well as enhance their own financial advisory practices.

Exhibit 3.11 | Financial Advisors Perceptions of the
Affluent Clients' Estate Planning Needs

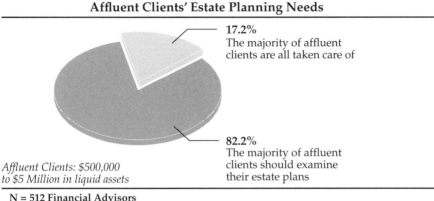

17.2%
The majority of affluent
clients are all taken care of

82.2%
The majority of affluent
clients should examine
their estate plans

*Affluent Clients: $500,000
to $5 Million in liquid assets*

N = 512 Financial Advisors

Asset Protection Planning

For at least 47.3 percent of middle-class millionaires, the topic of asset protection planning will certainly find a responsive audience. These are the affluent who are worried about being sued. Litigation can quickly and efficiently destroy the financial foundation of a person's life, especially if that client is on a less secure financial footing. This is a subject you might consider broaching with your middle-class millionaire clients. The need is there: Only 12.9 percent of middle-class millionaires have a formal asset protection plan (Exhibit 3.12). Like other estate plans, asset protection plans need to be updated (Exhibit 3.13). All of them were three years old or older and 56.8 percent were more than five years old.

Exhibit 3.12 | Middle-Class Millionaires
Who Have an Asset Protection Plan

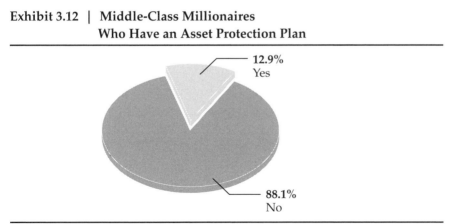

12.9%
Yes

88.1%
No

N = 1,417 Middle-Class Millionaires

Exhibit 3.13 | Many Asset Protection Plans Need to Be Updated

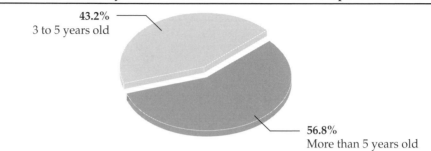

43.2%
3 to 5 years old

56.8%
More than 5 years old

N = 183 Middle-Class Millionaires

Financial advisors, meanwhile, tend to consider asset protection planning unnecessary (27.5 percent) or believe their middle-class millionaire clients have already addressed the matter in one way or another (51.6 percent) (Exhibit 3.14). Only 20.9 percent of financial advisors believe that their middle-class millionaire clients should seriously consider asset protection planning.

Exhibit 3.14 | Financial Advisors Perceptions of the Affluent Client Asset Protection Planning Needs

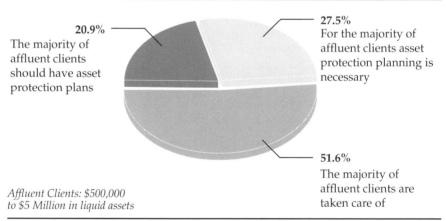

20.9%
The majority of affluent clients should have asset protection plans

27.5%
For the majority of affluent clients asset protection planning is necessary

51.6%
The majority of affluent clients are taken care of

Affluent Clients: $500,000 to $5 Million in liquid assets

N = 512 Financial Advisors

Once again, many financial advisors are off-target with respect to the extent to which their affluent clients have taken steps to protect their wealth from creditors and litigants. A pervasive reason for financial advisors downplaying asset protection planning is a function of their limited knowledge of the field.

Practice Implications

From financial products to planning services, there is a divide between the needs and wants of middle-class millionaires and what financial advisors perceive as the needs and wants of these affluent clients. Furthermore, financial advisors do not recognize the interest that middle-class millionaires have for private money managers, alternative investments, charitable instruments, as well as estate and asset protection planning. In effect, a great many financial advisors are missing the boat.

While we strongly advocate NOT approaching middle-class millionaires from a financial product or even planning service perspective, it is still essential to understand the significant financial product and planning service possibilities that exist. In *Part III: The Wealth Management Solution*, we detail an approach that has consistently proven to produce exponentially superior results than "hawking," or even adroitly positioning, financial products or services. At the same time, to make wealth management work as well as it potentially can, you need to have an understanding of where the opportunities are. And, the research findings point the way.

In thinking about your middle-class millionaire clients:

- *What financial products would best fit their needs and wants?*
- *What gaps would these financial products fill?*
- *What planning services are you well versed in?*
- *Which planning services make a lot of sense for your middle-class millionaire clients?*

Exercise #1 | Estate Planning

1. Returning to your ten very best middle-class millionaire clients, how many have an estate plan?
2. How old are each of those estate plans?
3. What has changed significantly in their lives since their estate plan was implemented?
4. What are the implications for your practice if they were to update their estate plans?

While it is highly likely that your ten affluent clients have estate plans, it is also highly likely that they are "stale." This would therefore provide you with an opportunity to help your clients while increasing your own prestige. The results are more loyal clients, as well as a boost to your practice's bottom line.

Exercise #2 | Asset Protection Planning

1. How many of your ten middle-class millionaire clients have a "formal" asset protection plan?
2. How would such a plan benefit each of one of them?
3. What precisely is at risk for each of the ten middle-class millionaires in the event of a frivolous lawsuit?
4. What are the implications for your practice if they were to have an asset protection plan?

In all probability not one of your ten middle-class millionaire clients have a "formal" asset protection plan. Moreover, for many wealthy clients, an asset protection plan is overkill where a good umbrella policy is sufficient. The key here is the viability of an asset protection plan for your more affluent clients. There is also the positive impact that addressing the matter with them would have for your practice.

KEY LESSONS

The insights provided by the research findings indicate, above all, the untapped potential of the middle-class millionaire market. For instance, the research tells us:

- Most wealthy people tend not to define themselves as affluent. Moreover, when it comes to social status, they see themselves as middle class. Hence, from our perspective they are middle-class millionaires. *You therefore need to recognize how they think about themselves and their wealth and not reflexively look at them as wealthy.*
- That said, net worth is the driving factor for a person's own view of his social class. Furthermore, net worth drives a person's financial concerns, as well as the services needed; yet, many financial advisors are in the dark when it comes to their affluent clients' total financial picture. *Instead of focusing exclusively on liquid assets, you need to also think in terms of net worth.*
- For most financial advisors, as well as financial institutions, middle-class millionaires are the "ideal" or preferred clients. This translates into intense competition for these affluent clients. *You need to gauge the extent to which middle-class millionaires are truly your "ideal clients" and determine what they mean to your practice.*
- Like most everyone else, middle-class millionaires are plagued by financial fragility. Most are living on the edge of the financial precipice and are very much in need of high-quality financial advice. *You need to be acutely aware of the extent to which your middle-class millionaire clients are balancing their lives and avoid making assumptions about their lives and lifestyles based on their level of wealth.*

One important finding from the research: There is a very big gap between how financial advisors perceive wealthy clients and how wealthy clients perceive themselves. For the most part, financial advisors do not really understand their middle-class millionaire clients. The research should therefore prove useful to most financial advisors by providing perspective. The findings should give you food for thought, enabling you to consider your middle-class millionaire clients and the opportunities they represent.

As we have mentioned repeatedly, it is essential to develop an in-depth understanding of all your affluent clients. Just because 12.9 percent of middle-class millionaires have an asset protection plan, you cannot assume your middle-class millionaire clients do or do not have an asset protection plan. When it comes to your practice, the statistics provide guideposts, but you have to move beyond them and focus on affluent clients as individuals. So, what you need to do is address the issues with them—avoid making presumptions. To be most effective in cultivating middle-class millionaires, you will need to be able to drill down as well as cover the waterfront with these wealthy clients.

The research gives us probabilities. And, as we can see from the results of the empirical analysis, there are many viable and profitable probabilities. Still, you will need to focus on each middle-class millionaire client individually. To this end we recommend a holistic and comprehensive profiling process (see *Chapter 9: The Whole Client Model*).

In the exercises at the back of each chapter, we asked you to focus in on ten of your best middle-class millionaire clients. What did you learn by examining these affluent clients? If you are like the greater majority of financial advisors, you found opportunities.

Many of the exercises ask you to return to these ten middle-class millionaire clients. When you have completed all these exercises, you will be strongly positioned to leverage your relationship with these affluent clients, improving your financial advisory practice—all the while serving them better.

So far, we have concentrated on sharing insights about middle-class millionaires based on the research. We have also shared research-derived insights about financial advisors. Going forward, we will continue to provide research insights. However, we will also be shifting to practical approaches —methodologies, tools and tactics—that you can employ to make your financial advisory practices centered on cultivating middle-class millionaires much more successful.

PART
2

CREATING LOYAL MIDDLE-CLASS MILLIONAIRE CLIENTS

THE VALUE OF LOYALTY

There are satisfied clients and then there are loyal clients. But there is a difference, especially when it comes to affecting your business. Imagine the impact a loyal client—a loyal middle-class millionaire client—can have on one's financial advisory.

- *On average, how many more additional investable assets do loyal middle-class millionaire clients provide their primary financial advisors?*
- *How does this compare with satisfied and moderately satisfied middle-class millionaire clients?*

As noted, middle-class millionaires are considered the "ideal" client for the greater majority of financial advisors, as well as financial institutions. Success, then, would be contingent upon serving clients well. If clients are served well, they will not only be satisfied, but also even develop a feeling of loyalty for you. And by loyalty, we mean an attachment that translates into a more profitable financial advisory practice. As you shall see, satisfied and moderately satisfied clients in general award more assets to their primary financial advisors. Oh, and satisfied and moderately satisfied HNW clients are more likely to go away completely than those who say they are loyal to their financial advisors. In sum, as you will see, loyal HNW clients are the kind who are not only satisfied, but so satisfied they actively talk about you to your friends, introduce you to them and back up the talk by bringing you more of their net worth to manage.

When we queried financial advisors about the loyalty of their middle-class millionaire clients, 79.3 percent told us that 75 percent or more of them were indeed loyal (Exhibit 4.1). Delving a little deeper we found that these financial advisors equated loyalty with perceptions like "having good rapport" and "doing a good job."

Exhibit 4.1 | Perceptions of Client Loyalty

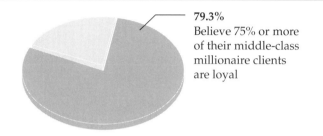

79.3%
Believe 75% or more
of their middle-class
millionaire clients
are loyal

N = 512 Financial Advisors

By now, you should expect that middle-class millionaires are not going to be as loyal as the financial advisors think they are (Exhibit 4.2). And, if you believe that most financial advisors have an inflated view of themselves, you would be correct. Overall, only 13.8 percent of middle-class millionaires would be defined as loyal to their primary financial advisor (defined as the advisor with the majority of the client's liquid assets). Another 39.3 percent would be defined as satisfied. That means the majority (46.9 percent) are only moderately satisfied.

It gets worse when we look across HNW profiles: satisfaction drops and so does loyalty as wealth increases. About one quarter (or 23.2 percent, to be exact) of middle-class millionaire respondents (again, those with between $500,000 and $1 million in investable assets) called themselves loyal; but, only one in ten (9.6 percent) respondents with $1 million to $2 million in investable assets said they were loyal; and, worse still, just 7.6 percent with between $2 million and $6 million said they were loyal.

The same trend is seen among those who are satisfied with their primary financial advisor. Of course, with so many of the less-wealthy middle-class millionaires satisfied with their advisors, there were fewer of them to be merely "moderately" satisfied. And, it stands to reason, since so few of the richest were satisfied, there were more "moderately" satisfied with their primary advisors.

Exhibit 4.2 | Loyalty by Investable Assets

Degree of Loyalty	$500K to $1M	$1M to $2M	$2M to $6M	Total
Loyal	23.2%	9.6%	7.6%	13.8%
Satisfied	48.4%	37.3%	27.6%	39.3%
Moderately satisfied	28.4%	51.1%	64.8%	46.9%

N = 1,417 Middle-Class Millionaires

The Value of Loyalty to Your Practice

By loyalty, we're not referring to the classic definition in which someone takes an oath of fealty, obviously. It's like that but even more measurable: Loyal clients translate into a significantly more successful practice. There are three ways to measure loyalty:

- Obtaining more assets from your affluent clients.
- Obtaining referrals from your affluent clients.
- Buying additional products and services from you.

There are two further measures to consider—the negative ones. That is, the probability the middle-class millionaire would:

- Take away investable assets from you while remaining a client.
- Leave you completely for another financial advisor.

Additional assets. In the previous 12 months, on average, each middle-class millionaire client gave $89,000 in additional assets to his primary financial advisor (Exhibit 4.3). Sounds impressive until you consider what loyal clients were doing: they were putting in the real money—$376,000 per client on average. The moderately satisfied clients added, on average, only $17,000 and the satisfied clients added, on average, $23,000.

Exhibit 4.3 | Additional Assets in the Previous 12 Months

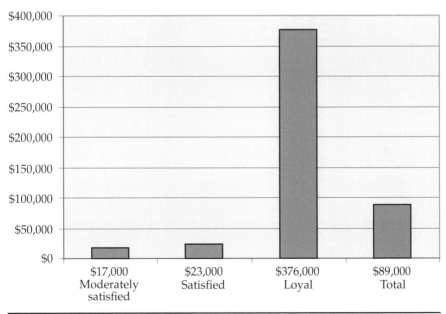

N = 1,417 Middle-Class Millionaires

Looking forward over the next twelve months, about a third (32.6 percent) of middle-class millionaires will likely give their primary financial advisor more money to invest (Exhibit 4.4). However, it is really the loyal middle-class millionaires that are driving this scenario (94.4 percent). Only a third of the satisfied middle-class millionaires (33.5 percent) and 13.4 percent of the moderately satisfied middle-class millionaires are so inclined.

Exhibit 4.4 | "Very" or "Extremely" Likely Within the Next Year to Give the Primary Financial Advisor More Assets to Invest

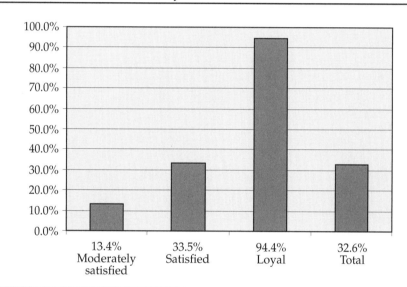

N = 1,417 Middle-Class Millionaires

Referrals. As we will see in *Chapter 11: Focus on Referrals*, client referrals are an effective way—if not THE most effective way—of building a successful financial advisory practice predicated on middle-class millionaires. Naturally, the goal is to win as many referrals from this wealthy cohort as possible.

Looking back over the previous year, while on average middle-class millionaires provided 3.3 qualified referrals to financial advisors, we find that loyal clients are an exponentially better qualified referral source than moderately satisfied or satisfied clients (Exhibit 4.5). A qualified referral is an investor with a minimum of $500,000 in discretionary investable assets who gave some or all of that money to the financial advisor to manage.

From 0.1 qualified referrals from each moderately satisfied client to 2.1 qualified referrals from each satisfied client, loyal middle-class millionaire clients provided 11.8 qualified referrals. For such clients there is often more at stake—personally, professionally, and emotionally—when recommending a peer to any type of advisor. Nevertheless, loyal middle-class millionaire clients are advocates for their financial advisors and actively look for ways to help them, including assisting them in sourcing new opportunities—new middle-class millionaires.

Exhibit 4.5 | Number of Qualified Referrals in the Previous 12 Months

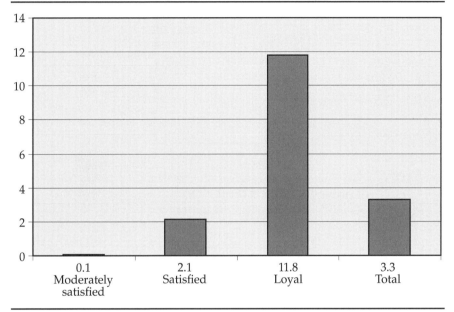

N = 1,417 Middle-Class Millionaires

Loyal clients refer their friends and colleagues and, indeed, skew the data. We find that, overall, 13.0 percent of middle-class millionaires are very or extremely likely to refer a peer to their primary financial advisor in the forthcoming year (Exhibit 4.6). However, these results are driven by the loyal middle-class millionaire clients, 81.6 percent of who said they were very (or extremely likely) to make a referral next year. Compare that to satisfied clients, just one percent of who said they would make a referral during the next 12 months; 2.9 percent of moderately satisfied clients said they would make referrals over that period.

Exhibit 4.6 | "Very" or "Extremely" Likely Within the Next Year to Make Referrals to the Primary Financial Advisor

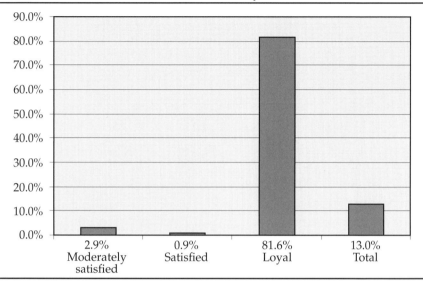

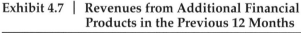

N = 1,417 Middle-Class Millionaires

Exhibit 4.7 | Revenues from Additional Financial Products in the Previous 12 Months

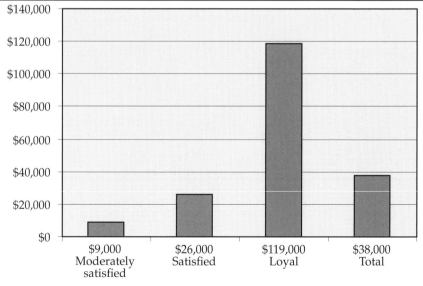

N = 1,417 Middle-Class Millionaires

Additional financial products. Overall, each middle-class millionaire generated $38,000 in additional revenue from non-investment product sales (Exhibit 4.7). We were extremely conservative in our analysis of these revenues. For instance, for life insurance policies, we assumed a preferred rating and a target commissionable premium of 70 percent.

Once again, loyalty makes a significant difference. The loyal middle-class millionaires generated an additional $119,000 each, on average. The satisfied middle-class millionaires produced about a fifth as much, or $26,000. Lastly, the moderately satisfied middle-class millionaires generated only $9,000 in additional non-investment product sales.

Looking into the future, 26.0 percent of middle-class millionaires are very or extremely likely to buy additional financial products from their primary financial advisor over the next 12 months (Exhibit 4.8). The same pattern we are now used to emerges, with 86.2 percent of loyal clients, 21.3 percent of satisfied clients and 12.2 percent of moderately satisfied clients very or extremely likely to obtain financial products from the primary financial advisor within the next year.

Exhibit 4.8 | "Very" or "Extremely" Likely Within the Next Year to Obtain Additional Financial Products from Their Primary Financial Advisor

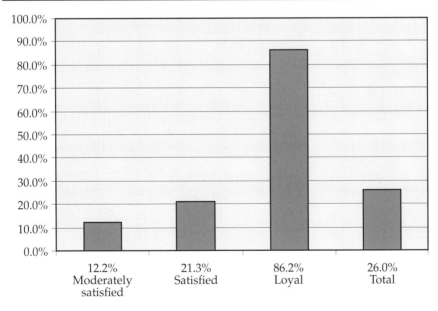

N = 1,417 Middle-Class Millionaires

The taking away of investable assets. Overall, 11.2 percent of middle-class millionaires took $100,000 or more in discretionary assets from their primary financial advisors in the previous year (Exhibit 4.9). Literally, none of the loyal, affluent clients took money away, but 9.8 percent of the satisfied, affluent clients and 15.9 percent of the moderately satisfied, affluent clients took such an action.

Exhibit 4.9 | Have Taken More Than $100,000 in Assets Away From Their Primary Financial Advisor in the Past Year

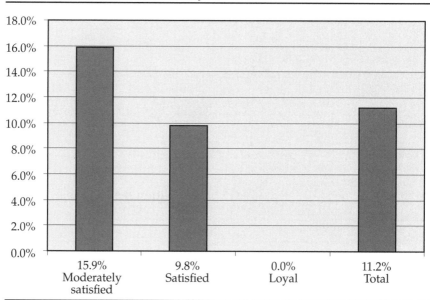

| 15.9% | 9.8% | 0.0% | 11.2% |
| Moderately satisfied | Satisfied | Loyal | Total |

N = 1,417 Middle-Class Millionaires

Nearly three times as many middle-class millionaires (30.7 percent) are very or extremely likely to move $100,000 or more from their primary financial advisor within the next two years (Exhibit 4.10). Once again, none of the loyal, affluent clients planned on taking money away, but 21.4 percent of the satisfied, affluent clients and nearly half of the moderately satisfied clients (47.5 percent) are likely to take such action.

Leaving completely. The extreme scenario is when an ACAT lands on your desk. In total, 13.9 percent of middle-class millionaires are very or extremely likely to transfer their portfolios to another advisor within the next two years (Exhibit 4.11). None of the loyal, affluent clients will likely be doing so. On the other hand, 10.1 percent of satisfied, affluent clients and 21.2 percent of moderately satisfied clients will likely do so.

Exhibit 4.10 | "Very" or "Extremely" Likely Within the Next Year to Take Away $100,000 In Assets From Their Primary Financial Advisor

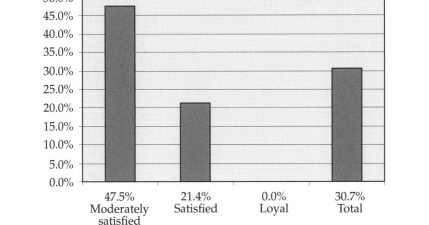

| 47.5% Moderately satisfied | 21.4% Satisfied | 0.0% Loyal | 30.7% Total |

N = 1,417 Middle-Class Millionaires

Exhibit 4.11 | "Very" or "Extremely" Likely Within the Next Year to Leave Their Primary Financial Advisor

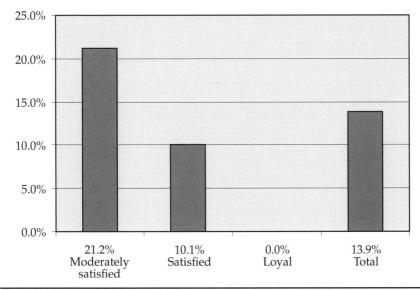

| 21.2% Moderately satisfied | 10.1% Satisfied | 0.0% Loyal | 13.9% Total |

N = 1,417 Middle-Class Millionaires

Practice Implications

Clearly, loyalty matters. HNW clients who are loyal mean more assets under management, simple as that. Loyalty results in more client referrals—the ones that turn into new (usually affluent) clients. Loyalty also appears to be critical if you want to provide non-investment financial products to your affluent clients.

At the same time, loyalty is essential in maintaining your book of middle-class millionaires. Put another way, the research shows that those wealthy clients who are not loyal have transferred investable assets to other financial advisors, and, even worse, plan to move more assets away in the future. A substantial number of them will probably leave their primary financial advisor altogether.

It is plain to see that creating loyalty is central to building a financial advisory practice predicated on serving the affluent. We doubt there are any financial advisors who do not want loyal clients; the real issue is how to move from having highly satisfied clients to having truly loyal wealthy clients, the ones who will talk you up and introduce you to friends and associates. As seen, there is a real difference between satisfaction and active satisfaction, which is essentially what loyalty is.

Consider:

- *How many of your middle-class millionaire clients are loyal as defined above?*
- *How many do you feel have the potential for being loyal?*
- *What are you doing today to ensure you have loyal middle-class millionaire clients?*
- *How is it working?*
- *How do you know how well your actions are working?*

Exercise #1 | More Business

1. Once again, of your ten very best middle-class millionaire clients, how many are loyal?
2. How much additional money did you win from each in the last year?
3. How many referrals did you get from each in the last year?
4. How many additional financial products did you provide each in the last year?

While there might be extenuating circumstances with respect to each of your ten middle-class millionaire clients, we have found that most financial advisors do not have many loyal middle-class millionaire clients, and, consequently, are missing out on an opportunity. Garnering more business from your existing wealthy clients is undeniably one of the best ways of making your practice more successful. However, relatively few financial advisors are doing this well.

Exercise #2 | **Triage Your Book**

1. Take the top third of your book.
2. Segment these clients into three groups:
   a. Loyal
   b. Satisfied
   c. Moderately satisfied.
3. What do you need to do now?

When we conduct this exercise with financial advisors, we find that, in general, between 80 and 90 percent of the top third of their book is either moderately satisfied or satisfied. They are certainly not loyal—and, as we have seen, loyal clients are key.

THE "6C" FRAMEWORK FOR CREATING LOYAL, AFFLUENT CLIENTS

- *What makes a wealthy client loyal to a financial advisor?*
- *Why is creating loyal, affluent clients difficult?*
- *What set of actions are essential to creating loyalty?*
- *What set of actions move you to a higher level of relationship management?*

In the previous chapter, we showed the importance of loyal middle-class millionaire clients to your financial advisory practice. From additional assets to manage, to more client referrals, to additional non-investment financial products, loyal, wealthy clients are so many times more profitable than moderately satisfied, or even satisfied, affluent clients. Moreover, loyal middle-class millionaire clients are not taking assets away—or leaving you altogether.

Obviously, what you need are loyal, affluent clients. What you need to do is take the proper actions that produce loyal, affluent clients. And that is where the "6C" Framework comes into play.

The "6C" Framework

As a result of our survey of more than 1,000 HNW clients, we were able to construct what we statisticians call a "structural, deterministic model" of affluent client loyalty. In other words, we were able to identify the various factors that produce loyal, wealthy clients. In the eyes of middle-class millionaires, the more you personify, the more you exhibit the below six factors, the more loyal these wealthy clients will be.

We were further able to determine how these factors interact (Exhibit 5.1), as well as how they contribute to producing loyal, affluent clients. In effect, we were able to determine which factors are most important and how they "work together."

In deference to financial advisors who have to make things happen with wealthy clients, we are motivated to sharpen the framework using Occam's Razor. This means we focused our efforts to derive the factors that result in 84.7 percent of the variance. In other words, we identified the factors—six in all—that will enable you to create loyal middle-class millionaire clients. These six factors are manageable and practical. If you were to try to go from 84.7 percent to 100 percent, we would be dealing with an unmanageable number of factors—41 in all. So, if you master the six, you will indeed create highly loyal middle-class millionaire clients.

The "6C" Framework is composed of the following factors (Exhibit 5.1):
- Character
- Chemistry
- Caring
- Competence
- Consultative
- Cost-effective

Exhibit 5.1 | The "6C" Framework

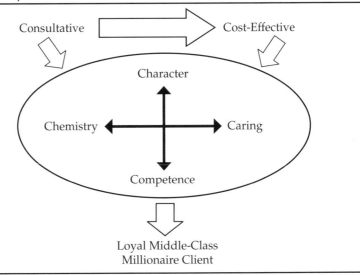

Loyal Middle-Class
Millionaire Client

Character, chemistry, caring and competence provide the foundation for loyalty in affluent clients. These four core factors can get you about half the way there (or, as we statisticians put it, 48.1 percentof the variance). Adopting a consultative approach is the most decisive factor, accounting for 41.6 percent of the variance. Lastly, 10.3 percent of the variance is attributed to being cost-effective. (We normalized the percentages so they would equal 100 percent.)

Character, chemistry, caring and competence work in lockstep. If a middle-class millionaire perceives you as caring, then you are highly likely to be perceived as having good character; the chemistry between you and the client would then be good, and you would also be regarded as very competent. As noted, these four factors are the starting point and the foundation for building loyalty.

That said, those four attributes do not mean you have a consultative approach (in other words, a non-sales, client-centered approach) in your financial advisory practice. Nor do they have much of an impact on the cost-effectiveness of their relationship with you. But being consultative dramatically affects the four core factors. Simply put, the more consultative you are the more you will be seen as having good character, that the chemistry between you and your client is exceptional, that you are very caring and that you are particularly competent. Also, by being highly consultative the cost of your financial products and services are seen as less of an issue.

If your products and services are seen as too expensive, then you end up slightly mitigating the impact of the four core factors. For example, if your service is seen as being too expensive, then you are seen as less caring and even less competent.

Character

Character entails the personal qualities middle-class millionaires desire in their financial advisors. One of the important personal qualities is integrity (Exhibit 5.2). All clients, to be clients, must believe that their primary financial advisor is not out to cheat them; that's a given.

The real issue is: "Do you have integrity?" If your answer is yes, how does your middle-class millionaire client know? What have you done that drives home this point?

Another personal quality is trust. Are you a trusted advisor? Once again, if your answer is yes, how does your middle-class millionaire client know? What have you done that drives home this point?

A higher percentage of loyal, affluent clients (98.5 percent) report that their primary financial advisors are especially trustworthy (Exhibit 5.3). This compares to 79.3 percent for satisfied, affluent clients and 68.3 percent for moderately satisfied clients.

Exhibit 5.2 | Their Primary Financial Advisors Have Integrity

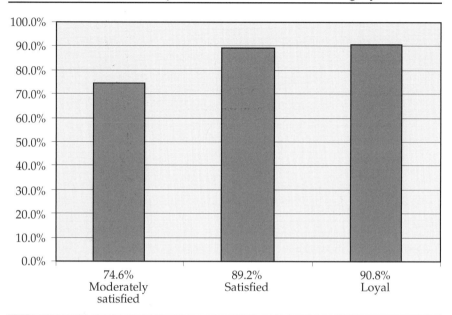

N = 1,417 Middle-Class Millionaires

Exhibit 5.3 | Their Primary Financial Advisors Are Trustworthy

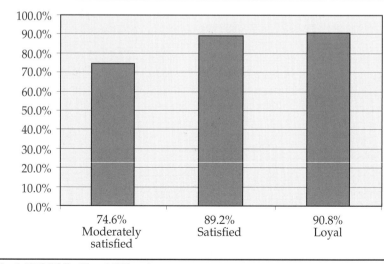

N = 1,417 Middle-Class Millionaires

Along similar lines, the greater majority of loyal middle-class millionaires (89.3 percent) see their primary financial advisors as being dependable (Exhibit 5.4). Relatively fewer satisfied clients (73.9 percent) and relatively fewer still moderately satisfied clients (63.5 percent) say their primary financial advisors are very or extremely dependable.

Exhibit 5.4 | Their Primary Financial Advisors Are Dependable

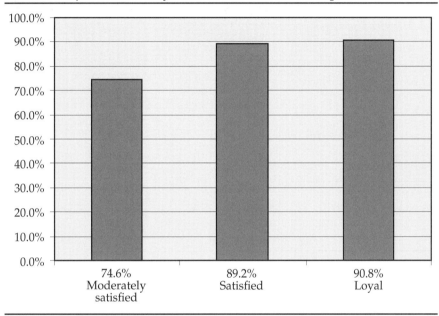

N = 1,417 Middle-Class Millionaires

When we talk to financial advisors about character, they all say they have integrity, are trustworthy and dependable. However, we have found that financial advisors have a difficult time communicating character to their wealthy clients.

Chemistry

Chemistry in the financial advisory business is a lot like, say, chemistry making a sports team perform together at their best; it's being "in-synch" with clients. You have chemistry when you "connect" with them. When it comes to financial advisors connecting with their middle-class millionaire clients, there is a sizable gap between those who are loyal (91.8 percent), those who a satisfied (71.4 percent) and those who are moderately satisfied [53.7 percent (Exhibit 5.5)].

Exhibit 5.5 | Their Primary Financial Advisors "Connect" With Them

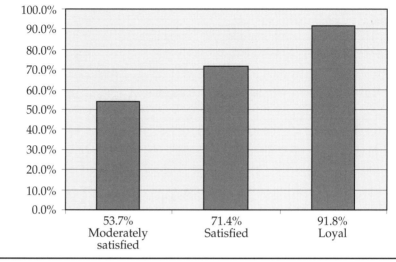

53.7%
Moderately
satisfied

71.4%
Satisfied

91.8%
Loyal

N = 1,417 Middle-Class Millionaires

Loyal, wealthy clients have primary financial advisors who know what they like to talk about [87.8 percent (Exhibit 5.6)]. Proportionately fewer satisfied, affluent clients (74.1 percent) and less moderately satisfied, affluent clients (47.1 percent) say this about their primary financial advisors.

**Exhibit 5.6 | Their Primary Financial Advisors Know
What They Like to Talk About**

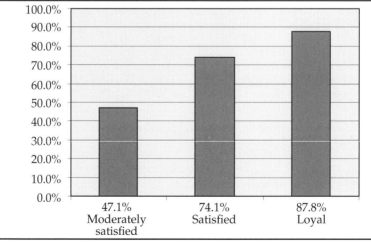

47.1%
Moderately
satisfied

74.1%
Satisfied

87.8%
Loyal

N = 1,417 Middle-Class Millionaires

Along the same lines, 82.7 percent of loyal middle-class millionaire clients report that they see eye-to-eye with their primary financial advisors on important issues (Exhibit 5.7). This was only true for 67.2 percent of satisfied, affluent clients and 47.1 percent of moderately satisfied, affluent clients.

Exhibit 5.7 | See Eye-to-Eye With Their Primary Financial Advisors on Important Issues

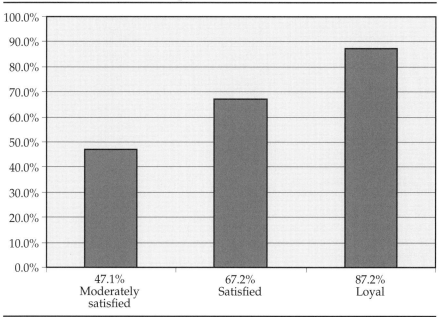

N = 1,417 Middle-Class Millionaires

Chemistry between yourself and your affluent clients is certainly important. However, it is the one factor over which you probably have the least control. Nevertheless, you can still take action to enhance your level of rapport with your middle-class millionaires.

Caring

Middle-class millionaires do not want to be seen as just the sum of their assets. In fact, a handful of clients—affluent or not—want to work with financial advisors who are really concerned about their well being. One powerful example of this is when their primary financial advisors put them way above making money (Exhibit 5.8). Three-quarters (76.5 percent) of the loyal, affluent clients feel this way compared to 65.0 percent of the satisfied, affluent client and about half (51.0 percent) of the moderately satisfied, affluent clients.

**Exhibit 5.8 | Their Primary Financial Advisors
Put Them Way Above Making Money**

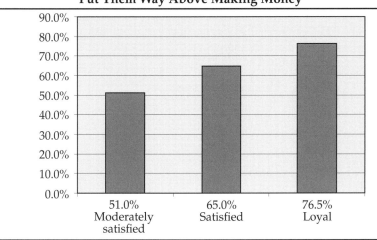

| 51.0% Moderately satisfied | 65.0% Satisfied | 76.5% Loyal |

N = 1,417 Middle-Class Millionaires

Caring is a central quality to the middle-class millionaire; you are a caring advisor if you take the time to know their goals and objectives. The greater majority of loyal middle-class millionaires (85.2 percent) say that their primary financial advisors know their goals and objectives (Exhibit 5.9). This percentage drops to 56.8 percent for satisfied, affluent clients and drops further still to 25.3 percent for moderately satisfied, affluent clients.

**Exhibit 5.9 | Their Primary Financial Advisors
Know Their Goals and Objectives**

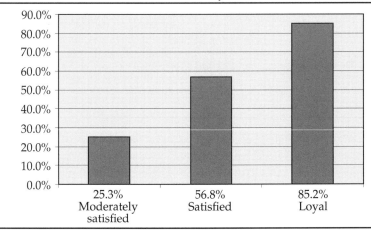

| 25.3% Moderately satisfied | 56.8% Satisfied | 85.2% Loyal |

N = 1,417 Middle-Class Millionaires

Similarly, 82.1 percent of loyal middle-class millionaires say that their primary financial advisors understand what is important to them (Exhibit 5.10). Only 55.7 percent of satisfied middle-class millionaires and 39.4 percent of moderately satisfied middle-class millionaires say this about their primary financial advisors.

Exhibit 5.10 | Their Primary Financial Advisors Understand What Is Important to Them

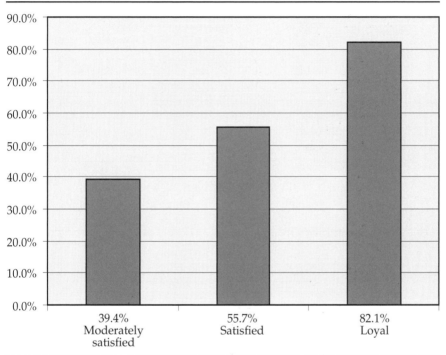

N = 1,417 Middle-Class Millionaires

Competence

The more their financial advisors can demonstrate and communicate their competence, the more loyal their middle-class millionaire clients become. About three-quarters of the loyal, affluent clients (76.5 percent) consider their primary financial advisors to be *exceptionally* technically capable (Exhibit 5.11). Satisfied, affluent clients (65.4 percent) and relatively fewer still of the moderately satisfied, affluent clients (42.6 percent) felt the same way.

**Exhibit 5.11 | Their Primary Financial Advisors
Are *Exceptionally* Technically Capable**

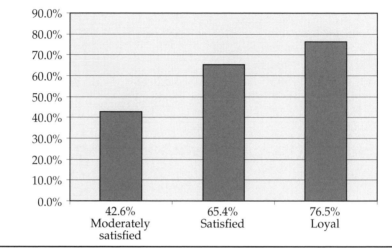

N = 1,417 Middle-Class Millionaires

As for their primary financial advisors being extremely smart, 70.4 percent of loyal middle-class millionaires feel this way (Exhibit 5.12). Meanwhile, 53.7 percent of satisfied, wealthy clients and 43.5 percent of moderately satisfied, wealthy clients also consider their primary financial advisors to be extremely smart.

Exhibit 5.12 | Their Primary Financial Advisors Are *Extremely* Smart

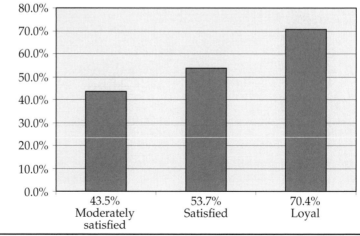

N = 1,417 Middle-Class Millionaires

A strong sign that wealthy clients consider their primary financial advisors to be competent is when they believe that their financial advisors are recognized as leading experts in their field (Exhibit 5.13). This was more the case with loyal, affluent clients (43.9 percent) than satisfied, affluent clients (30.5 percent) or moderately satisfied, affluent clients (16.8 percent).

Exhibit 5.13 | Their Primary Financial Advisors
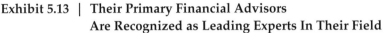
Are Recognized as Leading Experts In Their Field

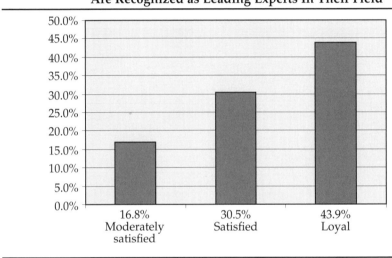

N = 1,417 Middle-Class Millionaires

Consultative

As noted above, being truly consultative is the most important single factor in creating loyal middle-class millionaire clients. Trouble is, it's easier said than done. Many financial advisors, as well as industry executives and consultants, laud being consultative, but few are able to detail just what you need to do to be consultative. To enable you to be more consultative with affluent clients, here are three of the central components:

- Cooperative orientation
- Contact parameters
- Customized communications

Cooperative orientation. Sadly, far too many financial advisors are trying to *do for* their wealthy clients. By that, we mean they seemingly act as if their job was to take affluent clients by the hand and take care of things for them. While this is indeed the case with some of the wealthy (for example, Phobics, see *Chapter 6: Positioning Yourself Using High-Net-Worth Psychology*), the overwhelming majority of the affluent prefer a more give-and-take relationship.

A cooperative relationship fosters loyalty (Exhibit 5.14). More than four out of five loyal middle-class millionaires (89.3 percent) report that their primary financial advisors *work* with them. This percentage plummets to 13.3 percent for satisfied middle-class millionaires and 7.1 percent for moderately satisfied millionaires.

Exhibit 5.14 | Their Primary Financial Advisors Work *With* Them

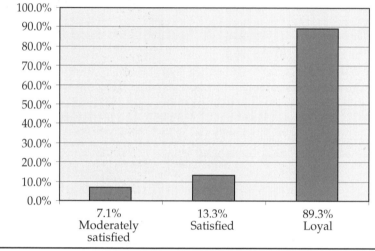

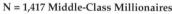

N = 1,417 Middle-Class Millionaires

Middle-class millionaires, for the most part, acquired their wealth because of their smarts—book smarts, business smarts or "street" smarts. It would be a big mistake to unintentionally rebuke them by not adopting a cooperative orientation.

Contact parameters. Most financial advisors see their middle-class millionaire clients once a year or once a quarter. In effect, these financial advisors are letting a computer program tell them when to meet with their clients. Furthermore, most financial advisors are busy putting out fires or prospecting or, (perhaps) managing money, and they unintentionally neglect to contact their wealthy clients.

Financial advisors build loyalty among their wealthy clients by contacting them appropriately (83.7 percent (Exhibit 5.15). Only 61.3 percent of the satisfied, affluent clients and 35.3 percent of the moderately satisfied, affluent clients say their primary financial advisors contact them appropriately.

Exhibit 5.15 | **Their Primary Financial Advisors Contact Them Appropriately**

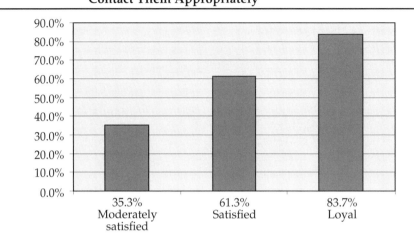

N = 1,417 Middle-Class Millionaires

What complicates the situation even more is that most financial advisors fail to contact their affluent clients on non-investment matters, and we have already seen how this is so important to being perceived as caring, for instance (Exhibit 5.16). This cannot be overstated: Loyal middle-class millionaires were contacted more than twice monthly (24.1 times) while satisfied, affluent clients were contacted a tenth of that rate (2.4 times) and moderately satisfied, affluent clients were contacted less than a twice in the year (1.6 times).

Exhibit 5.16 | **Contacted on Non-Investment Matters in the Past 12 Months**

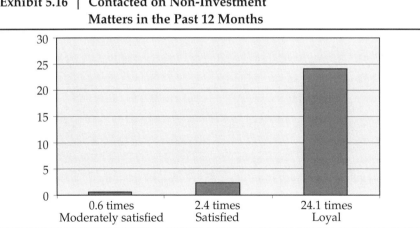

N = 1,417 Middle-Class Millionaires

Customized communications. Most financial advisors have their "shtick" and they stick to it. They go through their song-and-dance routine and it does not matter what else is going on. They can readily explain their "value proposition." They even have all sorts of handout materials to back them up. The only problem is that this approach is all about them and not about the client.

In general, the wealthy are looking for customized communications. They are not very interested in off-the-shelf presentations, particularly unsophisticated ones that come across as such. Still, most financial advisors use standardized communications for all their clients (Exhibit 5.17). Less than half of the loyal middle-class millionaires (43.9 percent) say their primary financial advisors are presenting data in accord with their preferences. Relatively fewer of the satisfied middle-class millionaires (30.5 percent) and even less of the moderately satisfied middle-class millionaires (16.8 percent) say their primary financial advisors are presenting data in accord with their preferences.

Exhibit 5.17 | Their Primary Financial Advisors Present Data in Accord With Their Preferences

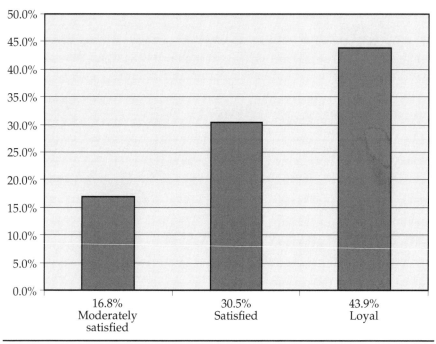

N = 1,417 Middle-Class Millionaires

To really communicate your message effectively, it is useful to spell out to clients the benefits that you are providing. One field-proven way to do this is by positioning your message vis-à-vis high-net-worth psychological profiles. This way you can customize your message by tying into the middle-class millionaire's financial motivation (see *Chapter 6: Positioning Yourself Using High-Net-Worth Psychology*).

Cost-Effective

Most financial advisors (79.9 percent) say their wealthy clients are pushing back on costs (Exhibit 5.18). They say this is forcing them to actually lower the costs of their financial products and services whenever they can.

Exhibit 5.18 | Wealth Clients Pushing Back on Costs

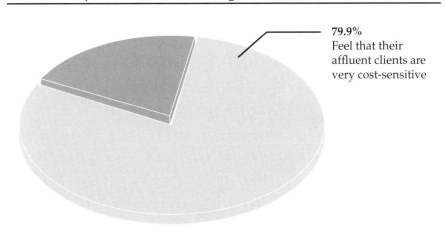

79.9%
Feel that their affluent clients are very cost-sensitive

N = 512 Financial Advisors

The truth of the matter is that it is not about cost. Loyal middle-class millionaires are willing to pay without debate for high quality advice (89.3 percent). (See Exhibit 5.19.) And, indeed, 75.5 percent of respondents say their primary financial advisors are not inexpensive, but that they are worth the cost (Exhibit 5.20). Predictably, satisfied and moderately satisfied middle-class millionaires question the value they are getting from their advisors.

Exhibit 5.19 | Willing to Pay Without Debate for Quality Advice From Their Financial Advisors

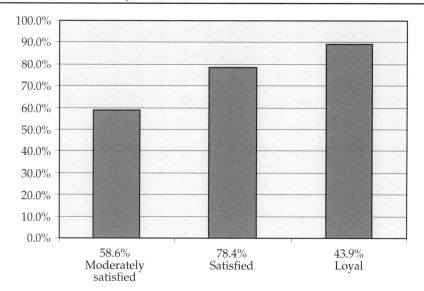

| 58.6% | 78.4% | 43.9% |
| Moderately satisfied | Satisfied | Loyal |

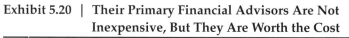

N = 1,417 Middle-Class Millionaires

Exhibit 5.20 | Their Primary Financial Advisors Are Not Inexpensive, But They Are Worth the Cost

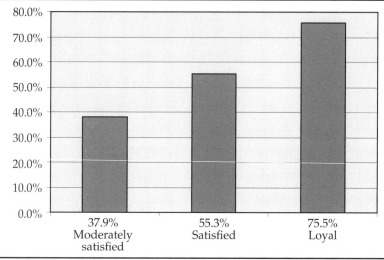

| 37.9% | 55.3% | 75.5% |
| Moderately satisfied | Satisfied | Loyal |

N = 1,417 Middle-Class Millionaires

For the most part, middle-class millionaires are focused on costs while financial advisors fail to focus on value. Middle-class millionaires, like most everyone else, are concerned about receiving significant value for their money. They want their financial advisors to deliver cost-effective solutions. This entails not only providing value, but making certain your middle-class millionaire clients know it.

Practice Implications

Each factor in the "6C" Framework is in your control. You can act in a manner that communicates caring, that demonstrates your competence that will make middle-class millionaires perceive you as consultative. You need to consider each factor and determine how to make that factor a seamless aspect of your financial advisory practice. As we saw in the previous chapter, loyal middle-class millionaire clients are the answer for a booming financial advisory practice. Satisfied middle-class millionaire clients are not going to cut it. And, don't even bother talking about moderately satisfied middle-class millionaire clients

As we look at the various factors, a pervasive theme emerges. You have to customize what you do for each middle-class millionaire client. You must customize how you explain financial products and services, and even modify your own behavior to ensure each affluent client is loyal.

With respect to communicating, high-net-worth psychology has nearly a ten-year proven track record of enabling financial advisors to more efficaciously position themselves, their services, and their financial products to affluent clients. This is not about changing the way you would create an investment portfolio for an affluent client, for instance. Instead, high-net-worth psychology is all about communicating the benefits of how you manage money for wealthy clients. We explain the nine high-net-worth personalities in the following chapter.

While high-net-worth psychological profiles can be quite powerful, moving to the next level, for you to ensure a truly consultative approach, as well as positively impacting the other five factors, requires a deep understanding of the middle-class millionaire client. We have already mentioned the value of the Whole Client Model and here again we note its central role in building a hugely successful practice based on middle-class millionaires, as well as wealthier clients (see *Chapter 9: The Whole Client Model*).

Some food for thought:
- *Are you consultative?*
- *What recent examples from working with your middle-class millionaire clients can you give that show you are consultative?*
- *How are you explaining the value of your offerings?*

- *How do you deal with wealthy clients who question the cost of your financial products and services?*

Exercise #1 | Character

1. Go back to your ten, high-quality middle-class millionaire clients.
2. For each, write down two examples where you demonstrated integrity or trustworthiness or dependability.
3. For each wealthy client, identify under what conditions you would be able to bring these examples into your conversations.
4. How would you use these same examples with other middle-class millionaire clients?

If you are like most financial advisors, the fact that your actions denote good character is great but not enough. You have probably not made much of an effort to proactively communicate the quality of your character to your affluent clients. Take the time and effort to hone your message and you will be able to build a loyal clientele of middle-class millionaires.

Exercise #2 | Caring

1. Identify five goals and objectives that are very important to the ten middle-class millionaires you have been focusing on.
2. Rank the five goals in order for each affluent client.
3. How are the financial products and services you provide able to help each of your affluent clients achieve their goals and objectives?

We have consistently found that most financial advisors have a somewhat myopic view of a wealthy client's goals and objectives. For instance, many financial advisors will talk about the fact that their affluent clients want their investment to make money. Just how many wealthy investors are looking to lose money? The real issue is "what do they want the money for?" Note: In the next chapter, we address the financial motivations of the affluent.

POSITIONING YOURSELF USING HIGH-NET-WORTH PSYCHOLOGY

- *Are all your middle-class millionaire clients alike?*
- *Do you tend to treat them as if they were all alike?*
- *How are you repositioning yourself, your services and your financial products based on the way affluent clients think about and "relate" to financial advisors, their products and services?*

High-net-worth psychology is a methodology for understanding what wealthy people want from their investing, as well as from you as their financial advisor. At the center of this framework are nine personality types.

Let's briefly explore the characteristics of each of the nine types of high-net-worth personalities (Exhibit 6.1). Let's look at the key needs, values and motivations for each personality. It shows what each type of affluent investor wants from his investing program. It answers the question *why* each group wants good investment performance.

Exhibit 6.1 | The Nine High-Net-Worth Personalities

Family Stewards	• The point of investing is to take care of their family • Are conservative • Are not very knowledgeable
Independents	• Exhibit drive for the type of personal freedom money makes possible • Feel investing is a necessary means to an end • Not interested in the process of investing
Phobics	• Avoid focusing on investing • Many have inherited the assets • Are confused and frustrated by the responsibility of wealth
The Anonymous	• Confidentiality is their dominant concern • Prize privacy for their financial affairs • Are likely to concentrate their assets and have few investment advisors
Moguls	• Investing is another way of creating personal power • Control is a primary concern • Decisive
VIPs	• Investing results in social recognition • Prestige is important • Like to affiliate with institutions and investment advisors with leading reputations
Accumulators	• The only goal of investing is to make money • Are investment performance oriented • Are fairly knowledgeable and very involved
Gamblers	• Relish the process of investing • Are very knowledgeable and involved • Have high-risk tolerance
Innovators	• Are focused on leading-edge products and services • Are sophisticated and like complex products • Are technically savvy

Source: The Millionaire's Advisor (Institutional Investor, 2003)

The Nine High-Net-Worth Personalities

In our survey, we found all nine high-net-worth personalities represented (Exhibit 6.2). Family Stewards dominate with 34.1 percent of the sample.

Next comes Independents (16.8 percent), followed by Phobics (11.4 percent). All of the remaining six high-net-worth personalities represent less than nine percent of the sample.

Exhibit 6.2 | Distribution Among the High-Net-Worth Personalities

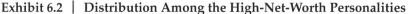

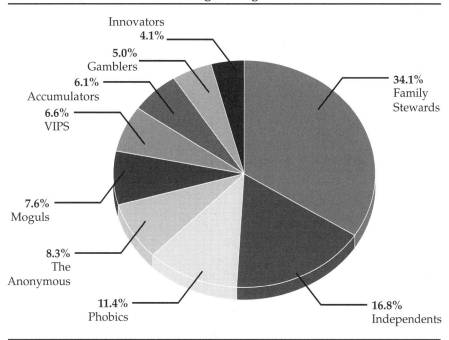

N = 1,417 Middle-Class Millionaires

Let's now take a more in-depth look at each of the nine high-net-worth personalities.

Family Stewards. Family Stewards invests in order to care for their family. The majority of their investment goals and financial needs will be linked to some larger family issue, like college funding or generational transfer of wealth. Family Stewards often will have privately held businesses, and they like to have their children work in the business. When asked what their goals are for their investments, a typical Family Steward might say, "Good investing lets me take care of my family."

Family Stewards are usually highly responsive to a variety of planning services because of their strong motivation to do the best by their families. They can readily understand why planning would put them in a better financial position.

Independents. Independents, as their name coveys, seek the independence and the freedom to do whatever they want. The way they achieve this is through financial security. They may actually hold a corporate job or run a business, but they aspire to being financially free to pursue a hobby full time, travel, or even start a business around their hobby (such as a tour company for cyclists). Independents are often characterized by having a vague financial goal that, once achieved, would allow them to pursue their dream. Once they achieve this goal, they do not always retire and pursue their dream full time. It seems that simply knowing they could cut loose at any time is the liberating feeling Independents crave.

Another area of significant interest for Independents is in retirement distribution planning. Independents know that once they stop working, their money has to keep working as hard and as intelligently as possible. This is especially important to Independents, because they are retiring early and will have a longer retirement, and a more active retirement. As such, retirement distribution planning creates another key issue for an investment advisor working with this high-net-worth personality.

Phobics. They are hard to miss. They do not like investing. They do not know about investing. Investing makes them uncomfortable. Furthermore, they do not want to learn about investing, and they tend to be adamant about remaining financially unsophisticated.

This trait of passing the responsibility of investing to the financial advisor makes Phobics a great group to have as clients. For one thing, they are the least sensitive to investment performance of any of the nine high-net-worth personalities.

Phobics are not interested in the various planning services. It is not that they do not need them—most do. But they are not interested in participating in an extensive financial, estate, investment or tax planning process. The challenge is how to get them to commit to a process they need, but do not enjoy.

The Anonymous. Did you ever have a wealthy client that took forever to really open up and tell you things you really needed to know? Or did you ever have one ask you "why" you needed their social security number? If so, there's a good chance that wealthy client was probably one of The Anonymous. It will usually take some time before The Anonymous will provide you with much information about themselves. The Anonymous feel that their money is their business and no one else's.

If you can secure the trust of The Anonymous, certain planning services are appropriate, in particular, tax planning and estate planning. A common theme with The Anonymous is anti-government sentiments. They dislike the government's knowledge of their financial dealings via tax returns, and want to pay lower taxes.

Moguls. Moguls are motivated by power. Moguls seek control, influence and, yes, power in their families, businesses, communities, and investments.

Moguls find the idea of asset allocation very appealing because it means they can have control over their investments without having to be involved in day-to-day details. Moguls are usually big-picture people. As such, they are interested in asset protection services because they perceive themselves as important, prominent individuals who may be likely targets for lawsuits.

VIPs. VIPs are status oriented. They like prestige and the respect of others. One way to identify them: Look around their offices for pictures of themselves with celebrities. These celebrities do not have to be nationally known figures; they may be famous only on a regional or local level.

VIPs are not very interested in financial or estate plans, as many already have them. Once you establish the general nature of those plans (and how recently they were established), you should advance the discussion to potential product. Down the road, you may find it appropriate to recommend that they review their plans, but do not push the issue too early in the relationship.

One of the VIPs' strongest interests lies in asset protection services, because they can see themselves as minor celebrities who may need to insulate themselves from lawsuits. They are also interested in charitable giving because they see donations to various causes as a way to elevate their social standing.

Accumulators. Accumulators save more than they spend. They tend to live well below their means. They do not exhibit any outward displays of wealth, and, in fact, have a disdain for those who do. What they enjoy is watching their pile of money grow. The more they have, the better they feel.

Accumulators are the most focused high-net-worth personality on investment performance of the nine. For Accumulators, capital appreciation is an end in itself. They do not want the money to do anything; they just want the money to grow.

Accumulators are open to various planning services, especially if those services will result in more money. For many of the affluent, and especially for Accumulators, it is not how much you make, but how much you keep. That is why planning services, like estate and tax planning, are of keen interest. Asset allocation services are also attractive because the point of asset allocation is to maximize long-term results.

Gamblers. Gamblers, as their "name" implies, love the excitement of the market—the drama of investing, the thrill of the big win. For Gamblers, investing is their hobby. For some it is their work, and for a few it is their life. Because of this they are much more performance sensitive than any of the other high-net-worth personalities.

Gamblers are very knowledgeable though they are not always astute. Gamblers believe it is possible to consistently beat the market and they like to recount their big victories. Not surprisingly, they often have a higher than usual risk tolerance. They will call you frequently commanding a lot of your time, but they tend to be active traders as well as long-term investors, applying a percentage of their portfolio to each strategy.

Most Gamblers say they are not particularly interested in having someone approach them with planning services, such as a financial plan unless it is truly state-of-the-art. For instance, consider sophisticated asset allocation modeling. Most asset allocation models deal only with investable assets. For Gamblers, you will need to deal with asset allocation models that incorporate all their assets, such as life insurance, real estate and retirement assets.

Innovators. Innovators, like Gamblers, are extremely knowledgeable investors. However, their orientation is different. Innovators like to be at the cutting edge of the money management field. They like new products and services, and sophisticated analytical methods. Innovators often have technical backgrounds, and might be computer programmers, engineers or mathematicians.

Like Gamblers, Innovators are interested only in the most sophisticated planning services. If you are conducting an asset allocation analysis, you should be prepared to review with them the various assumptions built into the model with which you are working.

Determining Your Middle-Class Millionaire's High-Net-Worth Personality

The approach to determining which high-net-worth personality you are dealing with is comprised of four opening questions, as well as a few follow-up questions. You probably already ask questions like these when working with your clients. However, what is different is that you will now be listening for something completely new. What makes this methodology work is not so much the questions, but rather learning to listen to your affluent clients' answers for the unmistakable traits of one of the nine high-net-worth personalities.

You will very likely not have to ask all four questions, just as many as you need. It may take only one to get an idea of a middle-class millionaire client's profile, or it may take all four and a follow-up. It will vary by affluent client. Now, let's go through the questions, and then show you what to listen for from each.

The four questions are:

- *Question #1:* "What would you like your investments to achieve?"
- *Question #2:* "When you think about your money, what concerns, needs or feelings come to mind?"
- *Question #3:* "How involved do you like to be in the investing process?"
- *Question #4:* "How important to you is the confidentiality of your financial affairs?"

Let's go through the questions and explain the logic. We will also see which of the nine high-net-worth personalities each question helps uncover.

Question #1: *"What would you like your investments to achieve?"* This question quickly exposes two of the high-net-worth personalities—Family Stewards and Independents.

Family Stewards are affluent investors whose primary life motivation is to protect their family in every way possible, including financially. So if you ask this question of a Family Steward, you will hear all about what they would like their money to do for their family, ranging from funding college education for children or grandchildren to taking care of an elderly parent to estate planning that ensures a harmonious division of assets for their children.

Independents will answer this question at the other extreme. Independents seek just that—personal independence. Their finances buy them personal autonomy, or freedom, the thing they value above all else. If you ask this question of an Independent, you won't hear about their family very much, if at all. You will hear about the dream house on the golf course, or sailing around the world, or about being able to retire at 55. Listen carefully, though, for the theme of freedom and independence—not about material possessions, like skis, golf clubs or a boat.

Question #2: *"When you think about your money, what concerns, needs or feelings come to mind?"* This question will help you identify Accumulators, Moguls and VIPs.

The key word "accumulate" will smoke out Accumulators. They are singularly focused on just one goal—accumulating more assets. Accumulators are not particularly concerned with what can be done with their money; they are driven to accumulate it.

Moguls and VIPs are interested in money because of what it can do for them. Moguls value money for the power it gives them. More money enables Moguls to have things their own way more often. They tell stories of affiliations and friendships with power figures, like influential politicians, that are not necessarily famous. Also, Moguls see themselves as power figures, even mini-celebrities, holding considerable authority in their families, businesses, and communities. Listen for these common themes from Moguls.

VIPs are status oriented. They like to be recognized and acknowledged. They tell stories about encounters with celebrities, and often have pictures of themselves with celebrities on their walls. They are interested in what money can do for them, but their examples will focus on material possessions. VIPs invest for what it can buy, and the lifestyle it can confer.

Question #3: "How involved do you like to be in the investing process?" This question is extremely effective in identifying Phobics, Gamblers and Innovators.

Phobics dislike investing; they are scared and highly intimidated of it. When you ask them a question like this, you will hear a lot about how much they do not like investing, how they are burdened by it, and that it is one more thing they have to do or worry about. Either that or they will attempt to change the subject completely.

Ask this question of a Gambler or an Innovator, and you will hear enthusiasm and commitment. They like, even love, investing. Listen closely to tell the difference between Gamblers and Innovators. Gamblers live and breathe investing. It is their hobby and sometimes their life. Innovators are not taken by the thrill of investing but by the intellectual challenge of it. They are technically sophisticated and like to be at the frontier, or cutting edge of the investing world.

Question #4: "How important to you is the confidentiality of your financial affairs?" This question is designed to identify one particular group, The Anonymous.

They are fearful and worried about personal security and confidentiality. They need constant assurance that you are protecting the integrity of their information as well as their investments. Ask this question of the other types, and you won't get much of a response. Sure, they want their dealings to be confidential, but they are not rabid about the issue. In contrast, The Anonymous are. They will explain how central this concern is to them, and how essential it is in any advisory relationship.

Confirming Affluent Client Profiles: The Trial Balloon

Once you believe you know which profile a middle-class millionaire client fits, consider floating a trial balloon to see if you are on target. Creating and floating trial balloon ideas are relatively easy. Simply follow the process in the flowchart in Exhibit 6.3.

Exhibit 6.3 | The Trial Balloon

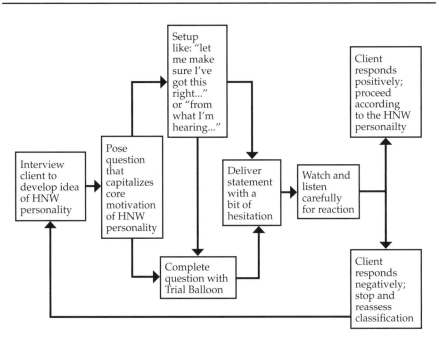

Graphic pg. 72 in HNW Psych
Source: High-Net-Worth Psychology (High-Net-Worth Press, 1999)

For example, if you thought someone was an Accumulator, you might say, "After having had a chance to get to know you, it seems to me that you are very astute about money. You know how to save it, and how to make it grow. I enjoy working with clients like you, and I'm going to do my best to make sure we create an investment strategy to make the most money possible." In Exhibit 6.4 we provide you with a trial balloon idea for each of the nine high-net-worth personalities.

Exhibit 6.4 | **Sample Trial Balloon Ideas**

Family Stewards: "... It seems your family's well-being is your primary concern. We are going to create a portfolio that's focused on your family, that's going to really take care of them in the long term."

Independents: "... It is really important to you to have the investment resources in the bank to make sure you have the freedom to do whatever you want. Maybe retire at 55. Maybe sail around the world. My job is to help you have that freedom."

Phobics: "... I get the feeling you are not that comfortable with investing. But that's okay because I am, and I am going to do my best to make sure that your goals are met, so that you do not have to worry."

The Anonymous: "... You operate similarly to the way I work with my clients. My key concern is that confidential information stays confidential. When we work together, you can rest assured that confidentiality is one of my highest priorities."

Moguls: "... I feel that you should be in complete control. My job is to make sure that you have the best advice and information in order to make the big decisions."

VIPs: "... It is important that you know we work with some of the biggest names in the investment management industry. People who are at the same level as you. People who know and understand the appropriate investments for someone in your position."

Accumulators: "... It seems to me that you are very astute about money. You know how to save it, and how to make it grow. I enjoy working with clients like you, and I'm going to do my best to make sure we create an investment strategy to make the most money possible."

Gamblers: "... Investing is exciting for you, just like it is for me. I love everything about investing. Whether it is finding a great stock, watching CEOs on CNBC or doing research on financials. Together, we can make sure we keep up with all of the events going on."

Innovators: "... You have a great deal of knowledge about investing, and it is very important to you to use state-of-the-art investment approaches. That's precisely what my firm, and myself in particular, specialize in."

Source: The Millionaires' Advisor (Institutional Investor, 2003)

Using High-Net-Worth Psychological Profiles to Position Asset Allocation Services

You are now able to determine which of the nine high-net-worth personalities you are dealing with. With this information in hand, you can more effectively position yourself and your financial products and services. To exemplify this, let's consider what you should do to most effectively position asset allocation services.

Before continuing, take a moment to consider how you have been explaining asset allocation to your middle-class millionaire clients. We have found that the greater majority of financial advisors have developed a concise explanation for asset allocation, such as "the systematic process of designing an optimal portfolio mix in accordance with specific risk and return parameters" or "creating an investment portfolio by diversifying into select asset classes so that the investment portfolio is properly situated on the efficient frontier." While these explanations are not incorrect, the real issue is how do they motivate a middle-class millionaire to work with you?

In order to garner the best results, you need to connect with middle-class millionaires about what is important to them and speak to them in their language. High-net-worth psychology enables you to achieve this objective. Family Stewards, for example, are not interested in the efficient frontier; they are interested in their families. Phobics are not concerned with risk reward parameters. Instead, they want someone else to take care of the matter for them.

In Exhibit 6.5 we provide examples of how extremely successful financial advisors have customized their explanations of asset allocations based on the nine high-net-worth personalities. What is important to remember is to customize your presentations in the context of high-net-worth psychology, as well as your own personal style.

Practice Implications

In *Chapter 4: The Value of Loyalty*, we saw the tremendous difference a loyal middle-class millionaire clientele can mean to your practice. In *Chapter 5: The "6C" Framework for Creating Loyal Clients*, we detailed the factors you can leverage that will result in loyal clients. High-net-worth psychology impacts each of the factors in the "6C" Framework to varying degrees (Exhibit 6.6).

Exhibit 6.5 | Sample Positioning Statements for Asset Allocation Services

Family Stewards: ". . . I know your top priority is to *take care of your family*. Let me tell you about asset allocation, the best approach we know for managing your investments so you can be *comfortable knowing you have done the best job you can for your family*."

Independents: ". . . I'd like you to consider asset allocation. *Because your goal is to be financially independent* and flexible, I think asset allocation would be a good approach to explore. Asset allocation allows you to *directly relate your goals to the way your portfolio is invested*."

Phobics: ". . . I know *you do not like to get into technical discussions* about your investments, so I'll keep it short. Many of the best people in the industry have worried about figuring out what is the very best way to invest: it is asset allocation. If you give me the go-ahead, *I'm going to have to look at what you have using this approach, and then we can talk again*."

The Anonymous: ". . . I've been spending time thinking about your account. There's an approach called asset allocation I would like you to think about. I would like to *prepare a confidential analysis for your review* next time we meet."

Moguls: ". . . I know you like to *control your portfolio*, and an approach called asset allocation gives you the *highest level of control*. With asset allocation, *you set the overall strategy and make the major decisions*."

VIPs: ". . . Because your portfolio is an *important one at this firm*, we want to keep you current with the kinds of investment approaches the *leading investors are using*. The approach, called asset allocation, was proven by modeling *some of the largest pools of money in the country*. We think it is something you should consider given *the importance of your portfolio*."

Accumulators: ". . . As you know, the very best way we know of today to *maximize your long-term investment performance* is asset allocation. Because *your number one objective is investment performance*, I think we should look into this some more."

Gamblers: ". . . I know you have been *reading the materials* on asset allocation I sent you. The reason I like it for you is that it is a way *of setting your aggressive risk profile* in the context of various asset classes. It will also require rebalancing, so you will have to *stay involved*."

Innovators: ". . . Our *technical experts have just added some state-of-the-art enhancements* to our asset allocation approach. I wanted you to know about these first."

Source: High-Net-Worth Psychology (High-Net-Worth Press, 1999)

Exhibit 6.6 | **The Impact of Using High-Net-Worth Psychological Profiles**

Factors	Impact
Character	Moderate
Chemistry	Considerable
Caring	Considerable
Competence	Low
Consultative	Considerable
Cost Effective	Moderate

Clearly, high-net-worth psychological profiles can be instrumental in enabling you to build a much more loyal middle-class millionaire clientele.

Some questions to think about:

- *What complications do you foresee in using high-net-worth psychological profiles?*

- *How can you overcome these complications?*

- *What is your high-net-worth personality?*

- *How does your own high-net-worth personality work for you in your practice?*

Exercise #1 | Positioning Your Investment Philosophy

1. For each of the ten middle-class millionaires you have been using in the exercises, identify their high-net-worth personalities.

2. Write a short explanation of your investment philosophy based on each of their high-net-worth personalities.

3. Now, write an expanded explanation.

4. How does your new expanded explanations differ from your original explanation?

Most financial advisors have a very well conceived and regimented way of explaining their investment philosophy. Now, the logic of using high-net-worth psychological profiles should not change the way you manage money or oversee the management of money. Instead, it is all about positioning—explaining your investment management approach in a way that strongly connects with an affluent client.

Exercise #2 | Positioning Non-Investment Services

1. Identify a non-investment service (for example, estate planning) you are comfortable with.
2. Write a short explanation of this service based on each of the high-net-worth personalities for your ten middle-class millionaire clients.
3. Now, write an expanded explanation of the non-investment service.

As with your investment philosophy or asset allocation, you can leverage your knowledge of a wealthy client's high-net-worth personality to more effectively position non-investment services and products. For many financial advisors this tends to be a little bit harder, but with practice and concerted effort you will become quiet good at weaving in the appropriate positioning statements based on the wealthy client's high-net-worth personality.

THE ASSET
CAPTURE PROCESS

- *On average, what percentage of your affluent clients' investable assets do you have?*
- *How do you know?*
- *What actions are you taking to gain a greater share of wallet from each of your middle-class millionaires?*
- *How effective are you in capturing more assets to manage?*

———————————

Middle-class millionaires with substantial liquid assets are strongly inclined to use several financial advisors (see below). For them, this is a form of diversification—a lesson they learned well from the financial advisory industry.

Despite this tendency, you can effectively gather a greater percentage of those assets from your loyal middle-class millionaire clients. Asset capture is important because it not only results in more revenue, it does so without

adding any substantial cost. Garnering more assets from your current affluent clients is akin to "picking off the low hanging fruit."

The place we need to start is with the research showing that the more investable assets middle-class millionaires have, the more likely they are to use
more than one financial advisor to manage their assets.

More Money Usually Means More Than One Financial Advisor

A tad more than 40 percent of middle-class millionaires have a single financial advisor managing their investable assets (Exhibit 7.1). However, we see
that this is heavily weighted to those middle-class millionaires with fewer investable assets—86.1 percent of them have between $500,000 and $1 million.
This percentage drops to about a quarter (26.4 percent) when we consider affluent investors with between $1 million and $2 million. And, if we consider
affluent investors with between $2 million and $6 million in investable assets,
only a small number (2.5 percent) use just one financial advisor.

Overall, a similar percentage (43.7 percent) of middle-class millionaires
use two financial advisors to manage their liquid assets; 12.6 percent with between $500,000 and $1 million in investable assets; 61.3 percent with between
$1 million and $2 million in investable assets; and, 56.0 percent have between
$2 million and $6 million in investable assets.

If a client has three or more financial advisors, he or she is typically very
wealthy. This is due, in part to the minimums many financial advisors have
set. For example, if you will only take accounts of $500,000 or more then
a middle-class millionaire with between $500,000 and $1 million would be
hard pressed to spread the assets among a number of financial advisors.
On the other hand, if an affluent investor has millions, then it is increasingly likely he or she will use multiple financial advisors to manage the
monies.

Exhibit 7.1 | Number of Financial Advisors

Number	$500K to $1M	$1M to $2M	$2M to $6M	Total
One	86.1%	26.4%	2.5%	42.1%
Two	12.6%	61.3%	56.0%	43.7%
Three or more	1.3%	12.3%	41.5%	14.2%

N = 1,417 Middle-Class Millionaires

Not surprisingly, there is a strong consensus among financial advisors
(81.6 percent) that, with respect to middle-class millionaires, they have ALL
the investable assets (Exhibit 7.2). Part of this is wishful thinking, but a more

pervasive component of this misperception is a lack of in-depth understanding by many financial advisors of the wealth of their clients.

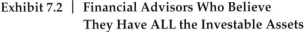

Exhibit 7.2 | Financial Advisors Who Believe
They Have ALL the Investable Assets

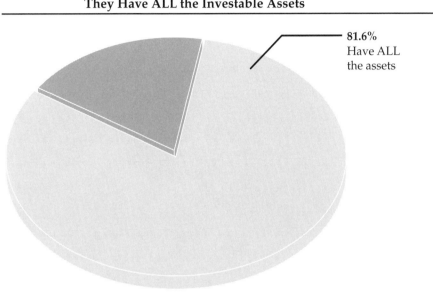

81.6%
Have ALL
the assets

N = 512 Financial Advisors

Financial Advisors Fail to Ask for More Money

If your investment performance is consistently outstanding, then you will tend to find that you will not need to solicit your affluent clients for more money to invest. Instead, they'll be happy to give you what they can. In this scenario, you are selling investment performance, and you should be aware that once your investment performance is no longer consistently outstanding, you would likely lose assets and affluent clients.

For the overwhelming majority of financial advisors, "consistently outstanding" is not the norm. If this is the case with you, then you are going to have to ask for more money to invest from your current middle-class millionaire clients. What stops advisors from winning more of their current clients' wallets? Very few (11.9 percent) financial advisors ask for more money to invest (Exhibit 7.3).

Exhibit 7.3 | **Financial Advisors Who, In the Last 6 Months,**
Asked for More Money to Invest

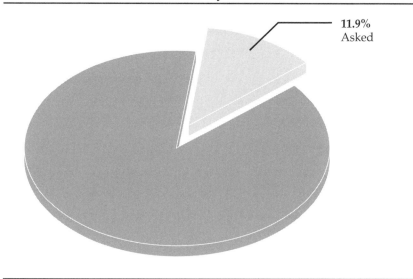

11.9%
Asked

N = 512 Financial Advisors

The biggest obstacle is not knowing how best to ask. Many financial advisors are uncomfortable. Which clients to ask? And when? Besides, as we have seen, most financial advisors believe they have all their clients' liquid assets. Since this is usually not the case, you have to learn how to be comfortable asking for more business.

The Asset Capture Process

The asset capture process is composed of four steps:
- Step #1: Create loyal affluent clients.
- Step #2: Identify asset transfer opportunities.
- Step #3: Ask for additional assets.
- Step #4: Say "Thank you" and reinforce the asset transfer decision.

Step #1: Create loyal, affluent clients. As we saw in *Chapter 4: The Value of Loyalty*, loyal middle-class millionaire clients have not taken assets away from their primary financial advisor nor are they inclined to do so going forward. Moreover, in the previous 12 months they provided, on average, $376,000 to their primary financial advisor and 94.4 percent of them are "very" or "extremely" likely to give their primary financial advisor more money to invest.

Exceptional investment performance is a factor in motivating middle-class millionaires to give more money (for example, be loyal). But for those advisors who perform only average, you can still gather assets from existing clients if you can add value in other ways; in short, make your clients loyal by using other services (as noted in prior chapters).

Step #2: Identify asset transfer opportunities. By and large, you need to ask for more assets if you want to get more assets. And, in order to do so, you will need to know that your middle-class millionaire clients do indeed have more assets that you are not currently managing.

As we saw, 81.6 percent of financial advisors believe they are already managing all the investable assets of their middle-class millionaire clients. We also saw that more middle-class millionaires—especially the wealthier ones—are employing more than one financial advisor to manage their money. So, you first have to believe that you probably DO NOT have all the investable assets of all your middle-class millionaire clients. Unless financial advisors approach the asset capture process with this perspective, they will surely sabotage any efforts to garner more assets.

There are two types of asset transfer opportunities. One entails finding a middle-class millionaire with a "pool" of liquid assets you're not managing and, adroitly, tapping it. Of course, you have to find this pool of money. The best way to do this is by having an extensive understanding of the wealthy investor (see *Chapter 9: The Whole Client Model*). Still, less comprehensive approaches are possible, such as estate planning, retirement planning and even broad-based investment management planning.

The other asset transfer opportunity is structural. For example, significant swings in the stock market provide you with an opportunity to talk to your affluent clients, and skillfully recommend they entrust you with more of their money to manage.

Step #3: Ask for additional assets. With only about one in ten financial advisors asking for more money to invest, the odds are that the other nine are not going to get any. Without question, asking for the business will do wonders for increasing your probability of getting more money. Simple as that.

In *Chapter 6: Positioning Yourself Using High-Net-Worth Psychology*, we talked about customizing your approach based on the financial motivation of your client. When you ask for additional assets to manage, you need to focus and position your services based on what is important to them—family for Family Stewards, personal freedom for Independents, and so on. So, in asking for additional assets, using investor psychology can enable you to better relate to your wealthy clients and consequently gain a "larger share of their wallet."

Step #4: Say: "Thank you" and reinforce the asset transfer decision. We have seen far too many financial advisors, upon receiving more money to invest, become very impressed with themselves; they fail to appropriately thank their client for the chance they have been provided. You need to let them know you greatly appreciate the faith they have in you.

Practice Implications

In spite of what most financial advisors believe—or want to believe—the majority of middle-class millionaires turn to more than one financial advisor to manage their assets. This is especially true the wealthier people become. Of course, part of this is a desire for diversification, one that the financial services industry promotes itself.

That does not mean you cannot increase your share of a middle-class millionaire's wallet; but it does mean that you will likely have to be proactive about doing so. Only truly exceptional investment performance results in asset transfers from existing clients with any regularity. And, asset capture due to market-beating performance is a double-edged sword. If you can no longer deliver exceptional investment performance, there's a very, very strong probability you will not only no longer get more money to manage, but you will also see net outflows—and suffer client defections.

Take a moment to consider:

- *What percentage of your middle-class millionaire clients have other assets you are interested in managing?*
- *What impact would garnering 10 percent of those assets have on the profitability of your practice?*
- *What impact would garnering 20 percent of those assets have on the profitability of your practice?*
- *Have you ever asked an affluent client for more business when your investment performance was not exceptional?*
- *If not, what does this tell you about the way you were thinking about asset capture?*
- *If you did ask when your investment performance was not exceptional, were you successful and why or why not?*

Exercise #1 | Asking for More Assets Using High-Net-Worth Psychology

1. For each of the ten middle-class millionaires you have been focusing on, identify where they might have additional assets you would be interested in managing.

2. Note the high-net-worth personality of each of the ten.
3. Specify in writing (no more than two or three sentences) how you would ask to manage those additional assets. Remember to appeal to their psychological investment profile in crafting your request.

It is very likely that your middle-class millionaire clients have additional money—even if it is only money in money-market accounts or demand deposits. Identifying those pools of money is often the hardest aspect of the asset capture process. Experience has shown us that, with dedication and practice, all high-quality financial advisors are subsequently able to derive customized and highly tailored ways of asking for more business.

Exercise #2 | Thanking the Middle-Class Millionaire for Giving You More Money to Manage

1. Let's presume that each of your ten middle-class millionaires has entrusted to you more assets to manage.
2. Write how you would thank them in words and actions.
3. Now, write how you would reinforce the wisdom of their decision to give you more assets to manage.

Thanking affluent clients is very important, if not obvious. Yet, many fail to do so. Reinforcing their decision to entrust you with more funds and doing so in a way that connects to what is really meaningful to them is core to being able to garner more funds down the line.

KEY LESSONS

Loyalty is core to building a successful practice serving HNW clients—the "ideal client" for the overwhelming majority of the financial advisory industry. Loyalty results in:

- Obtaining more assets from current, affluent clients, as well as mitigating the possibility of losing assets.
- Obtaining referrals from affluent clients.
- Obtaining, or a willingness to obtain, additional products and services from you.
- Not losing affluent clients.

The key, therefore, is to create loyal middle-class millionaire clients—a feat that can be accomplished by using the "6C" Framework. By being attuned to each of the factors and, with foresight and motivation, you can build clients who are not only satisfied with your service, but loyal.

Most important: Be a true financial consultant. By being consultative, you enhance all the other factors. You will be more readily recognized as having good character, as well as being very caring and competent. Your middle-class millionaire clients will also find that they relate well with you—that there is chemistry. Where there is chemistry and perceived value, there is less bickering over the price of your services.

A proven way to do this is by appealing to your clients' psychological investment profile. The skilled application of their profile will enable you to more quickly create loyal middle-class millionaire clients.

Lastly, it is very likely that you do not have all the investable assets of your middle-class millionaire clients. By implementing the asset capture process (based on their high-net-worth profiles), there is a tremendous possibility that you will be able to garner more money to manage—and do so relatively quickly. However, this requires creating, and working with, loyal, affluent clients.

———————

In this section, we delved into what it will take for you to build a loyal, affluent clientele. The exercises were intended to have you think through the actions you will need to create loyal clients by considering some of the middle-class millionaire clients you are more knowledgeable and insightful about.

———————————

In the first section we focused on research-derived insights. In this section, we addressed some of the "how-to" required to build a successful financial advisory practice based on middle-class millionaires. No matter what, creating loyal clients is a must. High-net-worth psychological profiles is a proven methodology that smoothly fits in with the "6C" Framework. And, the asset capture process is also a proven methodology for building up a financial advisory practice.

We are now going to detail wealth management. While not for every financial advisor, wealth management is probably the optimal business model —especially for advisors who seek middle-class millionaires.

PART
3

THE WEALTH
MANAGEMENT
SOLUTION

WEALTH MANAGEMENT AND THE MIDDLE-CLASS MILLIONAIRE

- *Are you a wealth manager?*
- *If you are, what were you before you became a wealth manager?*
- *If you made the transition from investment-oriented financial advisor to wealth manager, did your income (before taxes but after all expenses) increase by 35 percent in the first year?*
- *If your income didn't increase by 35 percent, how much did it go up, in the first year of your transition?*

Wealth management has captured the attention and imagination of clients, especially the more affluent ones, including middle-class millionaires. As a result, financial advisors have taken notice, too. It is clear that most middle-class millionaires (77.1 percent) prefer to work with wealth managers (Exhibit 8.1). About one-in-five middle-class millionaires (18.8 percent) prefer working with professionals who characterize themselves as financial advisors or financial planners. The remaining 4.1 percent of middle-class millionaires would prefer to work with an investment advisor or investment manager.

Exhibit 8.1 | Preference For Type of Advisor

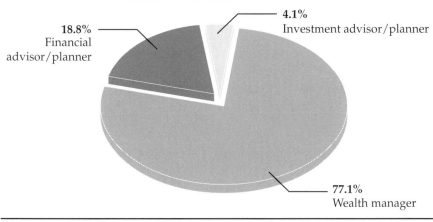

N = 1,417 Middle-Class Millionaires

Anyway you look at it, HNW people, as defined by either liquid assets or net worth, overwhelmingly prefer working with a wealth manager (Exhibit 8.2 and Exhibit 8.3), as opposed to a financial advisor/planner or an investment advisor/manager. We can conclude that the attention to the concept and "title" of wealth manager is very appealing to middle-class millionaires—especially the wealthier ones.

Exhibit 8.2 | Investable Assets And The Preference
For Working With a Wealth Manager

Type of Advisor	$500K to $1M	$1M to $2M	$2M to $6M
Wealth manager	68.7%	76.8%	82.2%
Financial advisor/planner	22.2%	19.7%	15.5%
Investment advisor/manager	9.1%	3.5%	2.3%

N = 1,417 Middle-Class Millionaires

Exhibit 8.3 | Net-Worth And The Preference
For Working With a Wealth Manager

Type of Advisor	$1M to $3M	$3M to $10M
Wealth manager	71.3%	83.8%
Financial advisor/planner	23.1%	13.9%
Investment advisor/manager	5.6%	2.3%

N = 1,417 Middle-Class Millionaires

You do not need the research to recognize the importance of calling yourself a wealth manager. These days it seems as if most everyone is calling himself a wealth manager. Indeed, in our survey of financial advisors, 77.9 percent refer to themselves as wealth managers (Exhibit 8.4).

Exhibit 8.4 | Calling Themselves Wealth Managers

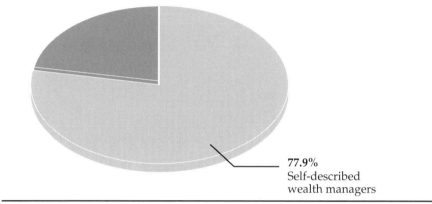

77.9%
Self-described
wealth managers

N = 512 Financial Advisors

Less Than Ten Percent of Financial Advisors Are Wealth Managers

While many call themselves wealth managers, few financial advisors actually do this kind of work. For the most part, their name has changed but their advisory practice remains the same. It's all too true: For many financial advisors the transition from investment professional to wealth manager came about by redoing their business cards. Other financial advisors took a bigger step and added a wealth management section to their Web sites. All in all, when we look at the research conducted with financial advisors, less than 10 percent are wealth managers—by our definition (see below).

In another study, we extensively analyzed the practice models of 1,177 financial advisors and found few wealth managers (Exhibit 8.5).

- *Investment generalists* offer a broad range of investment products and do not have a more comprehensive financial planning orientation (79.1 percent).
- *Product specialists* focus exclusively on an investment-oriented product niche, such as managed accounts or fixed-income or alternatives (12.4 percent).
- *Wealth managers* take a comprehensive, holistic approach in order to provide integrated solutions (8.4 percent).

Exhibit 8.5 | Very Few Financial Advisors Are Really Wealth Managers

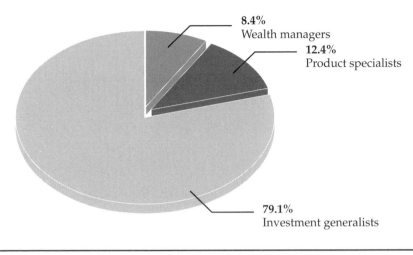

8.4%
Wealth managers

12.4%
Product specialists

79.1%
Investment generalists

N = 1,177 Financial Advisors

Wealth management is, for the overwhelming majority of financial advisors, the optimal business model. Unfortunately, few have made the transition, and it appears that only a minority of financial advisors will indeed become wealth managers.

Let's take a step back to make sure we are all on the same page. Let's define wealth management.

Wealth Management Defined

What is it? The term "wealth management" is thrown around plenty, at industry conferences, in the boardrooms of private client firms, in trade and mainstream articles and in front of clients. Yet, in fact, most financial advisors are hard pressed to actually define the term with any degree of precision. Based on a series of studies, we have found that most financial advisors tend to equate wealth management with investment management, often tax-efficient investment management. (Other more esoteric definitions of wealth management have included elements of the zodiac, astronomy and a wide variety of spiritual forces.)

Wealth management is very straightforward. From the client's perspective, wealth management is simply the science of solving and/or enhancing his or her financial situation. Any and all of these actions is accomplished by providing financial products. In effect, the middle-class millionaire is faced with a financial set of needs and wants, which a wealth manager can help resolve or improve by providing financial products. It's really that simple.

From the financial advisor's perspective, wealth management is the ability of an advisor or advisory team to deliver a full range of financial services and products to a client in a consultative way. That means, for instance, offering a client brokerage services as well as life insurance, estate planning and guidance when it comes to charitable giving. In so doing, the relationship is not inextricably linked to the ups and downs of the stock market. This tends to insulate wealth managers from being judged solely on the basis of investment performance.

Theoretically, a wealth manager can provide every single financial product in existence. In reality most wealth managers specialize in services and products they feel most comfortable with. Based on the research of the most successful wealth managers, the products they generally provide fall into the following three broad categories:

- *Investments*: including brokerage, fee-based accounts, derivatives and the like.
- *Life insurance*: for estate planning, business continuity and corporate benefits.
- *Credit*: from mortgages to business loans to personal lines.

Within each of these categories there are even more sub-categories. So, any individual wealth manager must make business decisions concerning just what financial products to provide, as well as how to provide them.

A further defining quality of wealth management is that it is delivered in a consultative manner. In *Chapter 5: The "6C" Framework for Creating Loyal Clients*, we showed how crucial a consultative process was to creating loyal clients. By being consultative, wealth managers are truly client-centered. A good wealth manager meets a client without any presupposition about what financial products or services are appropriate for that client. When was the last time you met with a wealthy client without any preset agenda about which financial products you hoped to get him or her into?

While it is common for a middle-class millionaire to be sitting with a wealth manager to address a particular need (investment management, say), the consultative wealth manager's overriding objective is to understand the client and find out what is important and why. Then the wealth manager is able to bring in the appropriate experts and provide the appropriate financial products (see *Chapter 10: Your Wealth Management Team*).

In sum:

- *Wealth management is the consultative process of meeting the needs and wants of affluent clients by providing the appropriate financial products and services.*
- *Wealth management entails coordinating a team of experts to address the needs and wants of affluent clients.*

The Rewards of Wealth Management

For most financial advisors wealth management proves to be the most profitable practice model. Wealth managers foster client loyalty (Exhibit 8.6). Three-quarters of the loyal middle-class millionaires (75.0 percent) consider their financial advisors to be wealth managers. Only 18.2 percent of satisfied, affluent clients and 7.4 percent of moderately satisfied, affluent clients consider their financial advisors to be wealth managers. And, as the data show, a wealth management orientation is instrumental in producing loyal, affluent clients.

Exhibit 8.6 | Wealth Management Fosters Loyalty

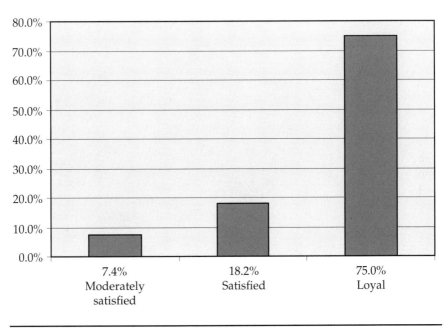

N = 1,417 Middle-Class Millionaires

Returning to our study of 1,177 financial advisors, we find that wealth managers have the highest gross production at $980,000 per financial advisor (Exhibit 8.7). The product specialists came in second with $510,000 gross production per financial advisor. And, the investment generalists had an average of $490,000 per financial advisor. Wealth managers tend to have more assets under management, but they have fewer (but wealthier) clients.

Exhibit 8.7 | Comparing Practice Models in 2004

Practice Model	Investment Generalist	Product Specialist	Wealth Manager
Average gross production	$490,000	$510,000	$980,000
Average assets under management	$26 million	$8 million	$71 million
Number of clients	330	210	80

N = 1,177 Financial Advisors

Without question, the specialist practice model can be quite profitable. As noted, the specialist is a content or product expert brought in by other financial advisors to address a specific affluent client need or want. For example, a derivatives expert is a specialist that would be brought in to hedge a concentrated stock position. Often, wealth managers will turn to life insurance specialists to help a wealthy client fix a situation involving life insurance, such as transitioning from private placement variable life insurance to a more traditional life insurance product because of a need for guarantees.

To succeed as a specialist you need a degree of emersion in a particular field that is uncommon. Thus, most financial advisors are highly unlikely to opt to become specialists. The other danger is that the area of expertise can become cold. A descending stock market, for instance, makes the derivative specialist lonely—and not very profitable.

In contrast, wealth managers are able to profit handsomely irrespective of the travails of the stock market. We have empirically discovered that irrespective of the stock market going up or going down, wealth managers, on average, generate greater incomes than investment-oriented financial advisors or product specialists.

Wealth management is exceptionally effective in enabling financial advisors to leverage their current middle-class millionaire clientele. Financial advisors are able to go to their existing affluent clients and be of considerable service and consequently generate significant revenues. For example, it is common for wealth managers to help affluent clients monetize illiquid assets such as, real estate and art works, or to put them into more liquid vehicles. So, a wealth management approach often results in more assets under management.

Taking a wealth management approach also turns out to be a very effective way to source new and wealthier clients. From generating a steady stream of affluent client referrals to creating a pipeline of affluent client referrals from "centers of influence" such as attorneys and accountants, the adroit positioning of wealth management is a very effective prospecting strategy (see *Part IV: Sourcing Middle-Class Millionaires*).

While we have considerable research showing the income advantages of financial advisors who are wealth managers compared to those that are principally investment oriented, the best example comes from those financial advisors we coached into becoming wealth managers. In one-to-one coaching situations, a financial advisor transitioning to a wealth manager will see profits increase by 35 percent or more within a year. This 35 percent increase is after expenses, including the cost of the coaching. Hence, if a financial advisor's annual income was $250,000 before becoming a wealth manager, his or her annual income will be $337,500 within a year (Exhibit 8.8).

Exhibit 8.8 | 35 Percent Income Increase

The 35 percent profit increase should be seen as the baseline. It is not uncommon for financial advisors to increase their incomes by more than 100 percent or even 200 percent after such a transition. And, most importantly, as we noted, wealth management results in much more loyal and better-served clients.

Wealth Management Is Not For Every Financial Advisor

That said, not all financial advisors are good candidates for becoming successful wealth managers. We have found that many financial advisors are doing quite well running money, for instance, and are not inclined by temperament or preference to transition into wealth managers. For some financial advisors, then, attempting to become a wealth manager is unwise.

At the same time, it is important to realize that wealth management is not for the overwhelming majority of clients. Wealth management is most appropriate for wealthier clients. It is very appropriate for middle-class millionaires. These are people with the issues and the money, as well as the needs and wants, that make wealth management a viable business proposition.

In doing "wealth management" with a client, you must develop and indepth profile. Doing so can take a fair amount of time. In order to spend that time, it only makes business sense if the client is appropriately wealthy; otherwise, he or she may not benefit from a number of the financial products you are able to provide.

In five years of coaching financial advisors to become wealth managers, we have found that about one out of 50 affluent clients cannot benefit from their expanded array of services and financial products. Thus, the odds strongly favor the wealth manager who is working with the affluent.

Practice Implications

For most financial advisors, wealth management is *the* solution that will ensure the immediate and on-going success—often times spectacular success—of their financial advisory practices. It is a practice model that has proven its worth in good markets and in bad, because unlike investment management, wealth management is sincerely about serving clients—especially affluent clients with complicated financial lives.

Wealth management as a practice model not only has tremendous business appeal because of its capacity to significantly leverage affluent client relationships, it has a powerful appeal for middle-class millionaires. Overall, understandably, the wealthy prefer to work with wealth managers than other types of financial advisors.

While more financial advisors are donning the trappings of wealth management, few—so far no more than 10 percent—are wealth managers in action and not just in name. For those financial advisors who make the transition to wealth management, the rewards are quite meaningful. As noted, the successful transition can result in a 35 percent or more increase in annual income. It also allows advisors to work closer with fewer clients.

To put wealth management in perspective:

- *So, how interested are you in boosting your income by 35 percent within a year's time?*
- *How hard are you willing to work to change your investment-oriented*

financial advisory practice into a wealth management practice?
- *At this point, what obstacles do you see inhibiting your transition to a wealth management business model?*
- *What can you do about these obstacles?*

Exercise #1 | Doing Wealth Management

1. Of your ten middle-class millionaires you have been focusing on, identify three additional financial needs (or wants) each one has.
2. What financial products and/or services would be appropriate to deal with each of the financial needs or wants?
3. How would you deliver and/or implement each of the solutions you identified?
4. In delivering these solutions, how will your income be affected?

Remember, only about one in 50 affluent clients are "all taken care of." This does not mean you will automatically be able to provide additional financial products or services. Just because they are not properly taken care of does not mean they will be amenable to your solutions. Nevertheless, you need to understand how they can benefit in order to be able to intelligently present options to them.

Exercise #2 | An In-Depth Knowledge of Your Middle-Class Millionaire Clients

1. For each of the ten middle-class millionaires you have been using in these exercises, answer the following questions:
   a. What is their net worth?
   b. What assets make up their net worth?
   c. Who are the most important people in their lives?
   d. What charities are they involved with and how involved are they?
   e. Who are their other advisors (by name)—accountants, attorneys— and how loyal are they to these advisors?
   f. How do they like to see financial information?
   g. What are their goals and objectives with respect to how they would answer "a" through "f?"
2. How can you use this information to appropriately provide additional investment services?
3. How can you use this information to appropriately provide additional non-investment financial products and services?

Based on nearly two decades of researching the affluent, coupled with extensive experience coaching some of the very best financial and professional advisors the world over, we have found that one of the biggest weaknesses is advisors' ability to *consistently* develop a comprehensive profile of their wealthy clients. This exercise can give you an indication whether you are the anomaly or more like the norm: There are some gaps in your understanding about even your close middle-class millionaire clients.

Because such an understanding is the cornerstone of wealth management, not to mention creating loyal, affluent clients, we now turn to one of the most potent methodologies for profiling the wealthy—the Whole Client Model.

THE WHOLE CLIENT MODEL

- *How well do you understand your middle-class millionaire clients?*
- *Who are their most important confidants?*
- *Who are the other professional advisors they employ?*
- *How important are their pets to your middle-class millionaire clients?*
- *What are the names of their pets?*

For most financial advisors, wealth management is the preferred practice model. Why? Because it best meets the needs and wants of clients, especially affluent clients; and because it translates into significantly greater profitability for them as compared to, say, an investment-oriented practice.

Fact: An investment-oriented financial advisor having effectively transitioned to being a wealth manager will see, at a minimum, an income increase of 35 percent. And, 35 percent is the minimum income increase in year one with 100 percent, and even 200 percent a year income increases not that uncommon.

The Whole Client Model is not just about wealth management. For example, say you are solely concerned with managing liquid assets. As we saw in *Chapter 5: The "6C" Framework for Creating Loyal Clients*, you will be able to build stronger relationships simply because the process demands that you actually understand your clients well. In so doing, you will be able to create loyal clients. And, we have seen these stronger relationships yield more qualified referrals and assets per affluent client. All in all, becoming proficient with the Whole Client Model is a solid way of growing your financial advisory practice.

As we noted in the prior chapter, as a wealth manager you'll need to create a psychological financial profile of each client. The profile reflects the client's needs, wants, facts, figures, attitudes, perceptions, and preferences about money and investing. In addition, you'll need to gather information on their other advisors as well as non-advisor relationships and understand their social dynamics.

A Comprehensive Profiling Approach

In the world of financial advisors, there are about as many fact-finders (profile questionnaires) as there are advisors to the affluent. Unfortunately, most fact-finders tend to be skewed by their narrow focus on the assets and related financial information. Such assessments offer exhaustive detail about the wealthy person's various classes of assets. Most of these assessments do not, however, adequately sum up an affluent client's financial life and, therefore, may not help the wealth manager identify and create proper solutions.

To create a more accurate, perceptive and actionable fact-finder, we distilled the components of the client profile into seven categories referred to as the Whole Client Model. The following is the seven-sector framework, along with sample questions:

Client

- What is the client's age?
- What is the client's total net worth?
- What is the client's gender?
- What is the client's income?
- What is the client's high-net-worth personality?

Goals and Concerns

- What are the client's lifestyle desires? (for example, houses, travel, boats, cars?)
- What does the client consider his or her top accomplishments to be? What would he or she like them to be?
- What are the client's personal goals? What is of central importance to the client personally?
- What keeps clients up at night? In other words, what worries the client?
- What are the client's professional goals (short and long-term)?

- What does the client do for his or her children? What does the client want to do?
- What does the client do for his or her parents? What does the client want to do?
- What does the client do or want to do for other family members or close friends?
- What does the client want to do for society, for the world at large?
- Ideally, where would the client like to be when he or she is 45? And then at age 55, 65 and 75?
- What are the client's investment goals? In dollar figures, how much money does he or she need or want?
- If the client did not have to work anymore, what would he or she do?

Relationships

- What family member relationships (spouse, children, brothers, sisters, parents, *et al.*) are the most important ones? Are any family members important in the client's professional life?
- What is the client's religious orientation? How devout is he or she?
- What pets does the client have? How important are these pets?
- How important are the relationships with the people the client works with?
- How important to the client are relationships with people in the community?
- Would the client describe him or herself as an introvert or extrovert?
- What famous people does the client know? How did he or she meet them?
- What schools did the client go to? How important is his or her relationship with these schools?

Financials

- What does the client's investment portfolio look like today?
- How are the non-investable assets structured?
- How does the client make money today? How is that likely to change in the next three years?
- How does the client save or set aside money to invest? How is this likely to change in the next three years?
- What benefits does the client receive from his or her workplace?
- What life insurance does the client have?
- What property does the client have (for example, real property, art, jewelry, etc.)?
- What new assets does the client expect to receive (for example, inheritances, stock options) and when?
- What is the client's opinion on taxes? What kinds of taxes bother the

client the most?
- What are his or her three biggest worries about his or her investment portfolio?
- What were the client's best and worst investments? What happened?
- What is the client's debt situation?

Advisors

- Who are the other advisors the client is using? What role does each play?
- How frequently has the client switched advisors?
- What was the client's best and worst experience with an advisor?
- Does the client have a trusts and estates lawyer? How does he or she feel about the relationship?
- Does the client have a life insurance agent? How does he or she feel about the relationship?
- Does the client have an accountant? How does he or she feel about the relationship?
- Does the client have investment advisors? How does he or she feel about these relationships?
- Does the client have a financial planner? How does he or she feel about the relationship?

Process

- How many contacts are optimal for the client? Investment-oriented contacts? Noninvestment-oriented contacts?
- What security measures is the client using to protect his or her personal and financial information?
- Who else needs to be involved in the planning process for the client?
- How many face-to-face meetings would the client want over the course of a year?
- Would the client want a call from you when there is a sudden change in the market?
- Does the client want e-mail contacts from you? What should the e-mail contacts be about?
- How often does the client want an overall review of his or her financial situation and progress toward goals?

Interests

- What are the client's favorite activities, TV programs, movies and sport teams?
- Is health and fitness important to the client? If so, what is his or her regimen?
- What charitable causes does the client donate to? Does he or she

volunteer?
- What does the client enjoy reading?
- What are the client's hobbies?
- What would the client's ideal weekend be?
- What would an ideal vacation be?

As noted, these are just sample questions drawn from hundreds used by top-flight wealth managers with their affluent clients. Of course, you would not use all of them; you will end up finding questions that work best for you and fold them into your own list. The actual questions you use are not important; what is important is that you realize the type of information you need to obtain.

Whatever the means, just get the information on one page, because it will enable you to see the inter-relationships. You'll better understand which financial products and services to recommend. The way we do this is by using a modified mind-mapping approach (Exhibit 9.1).

Exhibit 9.1 | The Whole Client Model Graphic

There are major advantages to using this graphic approach to organizing data than mere note taking. A few of the key advantages of using this modified, mind-mapping approach include:

- You can organize the information more rapidly and effectively.
- You can more easily recognize fact-patterns based on multiple pieces of information.
- You can better communicate what the middle-class millionaire client is all about to the specialists who are on your wealth management team.

The center category is the client. Then other six categories are vectors off the center. In conversing with the middle-class millionaire you would, over time, work to gather detailed information with respect to each category. This does not happen in one meeting; a comprehensive profile will usually take several meetings. For example, if the middle-class millionaire client best fits the Anonymous profile, it will take you quite some time before he or she opens up about many of these issues. Even with respect to the other high-net-worth personalities, you should recognize that they are inclined to move slowly—their trust must be earned over time.

The Rationale of the Seven Categories of the Whole Client Model

The Whole Client Model is essential in unearthing information that often translates into comprehensive client profiles. This will help guide the way to the opportunities for the provisioning of financial products. Without such a broad based and intense approach financial advisors may very well be doing their affluent clients a disservice by not being able to bring to them financial products and services that could truly benefit them. Why this failing? Because they do not see all the dots and therefore will not be able to properly connect them.

What the Whole Client Model does is provide wealth managers with an especially effectual way to examine an affluent client's life, dreams, fears, aspirations and reservations. With these insights in hand, the wealth manager can then select various potential financial products and services. The advisor can also select the suitable experts (see *Chapter 10: Your Wealth Management Team*) to help create an appropriate solution. Furthermore, because of the "Process" category, the wealth manager is able to present these options in a manner the affluent client will be most receptive to.

The seven categories cover the waterfront. That is, by employing the Whole Client Model, you are addressing an affluent client's panoply of life/wealth issues. As you drill down in each category, you are learning what is and is not meaningful to him or her. Again, this will help you determine which financial products and services are best for each individual.

In examining the logic behind the seven categories, we see that:

- The *Client* category provides wealth managers key demographic and psychographic information about the affluent individual.
- *Goals and Concerns* enable wealth managers to focus on those actions that will achieve the "true" agenda of the affluent client.
- The *Relationships* category informs wealth managers not only who is important, but how they are important. This category often provides insight into who might need to play a role in the affluent client's decision-making process.
- The *Financials* category is the most straightforward and the one the majority of financial advisors are most comfortable with. However, this category takes on a different texture in the context of the entire profiling process.
- *Advisors*, an often overlooked but critical category, provides insight on both how to structure a relationship with an affluent client, as well as what other professionals might be important to bring into selected discussions.
- *Process* is rarely examined in appropriate detail—or examined at all—and can often motivate or deter the wealthy client to take action.
- *Interests* usually prove instrumental in crafting the various solutions along with building rapport.

A Matter of "Values"

Occasionally, financial advisors will ask about the values of their wealthy client. If so, why don't we have a category called Values? First of all, a middle-class millionaire's values are very important; they underpin much of their intentions and actions.

Asking about values is tricky. We do not recommend that you directly ask them about their values. Why? Because when people are questioned about their values, they tend to give socially correct responses, answers that they think they should provide. To be able to deliver the best wealth management solutions to a middle-class millionaire client, you need reality not fantasies.

When you become proficient with the Whole Client Model, you will find that your affluent client's values are as visible as a 50-foot neon sign in a ten-foot room. By employing the Whole Client Model, the affluent client's values are ascertained unobtrusively and without any filtering. You will be able to determine their values from their high-net-worth personality profiles, from their goals and concerns, from their interests and from the nature of their personal and professional relationships.

Playing the Odds

It is essential to approach each middle-class millionaire as a unique person with unique needs and issues. At the same time, you would be wise to play the odds. By that we mean taking advantage of the probability that the unique middle-class millionaire client you are talking to has issues and problems that many of their peers face. Consequently, they might need some of the same (or slightly customized) solutions that your other HNW clients use. Moreover, they are middle class and are going to share the values of others who also see themselves as middle class.

The research we detailed in **Part I: The Middle-Class Millionaire** can be quite useful in helping you frame your line of questioning when talking with your affluent clients. For example, the fact that your wealthy clients consider themselves middle class speaks volumes about them.

It is highly likely that your middle-class millionaire clients are plagued by financial fragility, as are 88.6 percent of our respondents. You need to determine if this is the case with your wealthy clients and then what that means to him. Thus, your recommendations will be more on target, and you will be able to tie your suggestion back to a critical concern of the affluent client's.

These insights can effectively provide you with ways to shape your questions. They can help you by giving you trial balloons that can enable you to test hypotheses as well as move the conversation along. Moreover, they are very useful in making sure you touch on issues that are likely to elicit a positive response.

Lessons From the Field

With appropriate commitment and practice, most any financial advisor can become quite proficient using the Whole Client Model. Still, in coaching financial advisors to become wealth managers, we have found a number of common speed bumps when it comes to gaining proficiency with the Whole Client Model.

These speed bumps come in two varieties. One is in the approach. The other entails the all too common mistakes in questioning the affluent client.

The approach. We have found, and continue to find, that many financial advisors have been so well trained in how to gather data that they revert to this approach instinctively. However, when it comes to the Whole Client Model, there tend to be some differences in approach that can prove problematic unless you adjust (Exhibit 9.2).

Always remember you are not going to the meeting to sell the middle-class millionaire. You are a marketer; you're not a salesperson. You need to be flexible and openminded. You are looking to uncover issues and then ways for you to deliver meaningful value to address those issues. When you are pitching a financial product or service and that product or service does not resonate with the affluent client, you have struck out and might not have another turn at bat.

When you meet with middle-class millionaire clients to employ the Whole Client Model, it is all about them. You should bring as little in the way of marketing material—including pitch books—as possible to the meeting. The more you can keep the meeting centered on the affluent client, the more successful you will be.

By most yardsticks, middle-class millionaires are in fact quite rich (although they might not consider themselves rich). They want to work with professionals. Professionals do not come to a meeting with forms to fill out and a paper with a list of questions on it they need to consult. You must become proficient with the Whole Client Model so that you can employ it with just a pen and a sheet of paper. By working this way, you will convey a higher degree of professionalism.

We have seen many financial advisors new to the Whole Client Model try very hard to obtain all the information from an affluent client in order to fill out the graphic. When this happens, you have regressed back to what you do not want to do. You want to let the wealthy client lead the discussion; wherever it goes, you follow. Over time, you will fill in the graphic.

Getting together again to talk is not a good next step. But getting another meeting for two weeks hence to introduce them to a trusts and estates lawyer is a good next step. A wealth manager should think of himself as being a project manager. You have to keep the affluent client engaged, manage the interactions with all the appropriate specialists and keep everything moving forward. This requires strong organizational skills. After each and every meeting, you must identify the next step.

Exhibit 9.2 | Do's & Don'ts

Do's	Don'ts
Go to the affluent client meeting flexible and openminded, looking for ways to provide value to the affluent client	Go looking to make a sale
Bring as few materials as possible	Come with a pitch book and/or lots of handouts about yourself
Use a blank sheet of paper to collect the information	Have a list of questions and/or forms at the ready
Let the affluent client lead the discussion	Try to get all the information to fill out the graphic
Leave the meeting with clearly articulated "next steps," including a timeline	Leave the "next steps" vague

Category complications. Another place financial advisors often stumble centers around the seven categories. This obstacle is regularly surmounted by practice and attention to detail. What follows are some of the oversights many financial advisors make:

Client

- Not capturing net-worth information and only looking for liquid assets.
- Forgetting to identify the middle-class millionaire's high-net-worth personality.

Goals and Concerns

- Misreading goals.
- Failing to help identify key concerns.

Relationships

- Failing to realize the middle-class millionaire cares about other people outside his or her immediate family.
- Failing to identify important relationships with people outside their family.

Financials

- Not identifying all the assets.
- Not identifying the liabilities.

Advisors

- Not getting any details about the other advisors.
- Not finding the degree to which these other advisors are still relevant.

Process

- Not delving deep enough into the way they process information.
- Not finding out whom in their world can expedite or derail progress.

Interests

- Not determining the client's charitable activities, even if it's only "checkbook" charity.
- Not delving deep enough to find personal interests even if the affluent

client is a workaholic.

You might never have any difficulties applying the Whole Client Model, or, if you are like most financial advisors, there will be some glitches that will take a little persistence to overcome. These examples tend to be some of the most common mistakes.

The Whole Client Model and Affluent Client Loyalty

By using the Whole Client Model, you develop a much more intimate and intense relationship with your middle-class millionaire clients. Such a close relationship goes a long way to creating loyal affluent clients. In fact, the Whole Client Model can positively impact each of the factors in the "6C" Framework (Exhibit 9.3). Of course, to have an impact you will have to leverage the knowledge and insights you have obtained about the affluent client.

If you are effectively employing the Whole Client Model, your strongest impact will be on the most important factor—being consultative (rating of 9.6 out of 10). You can also achieve ratings above 9 for Caring (9.3) and Chemistry (9.1). Using the Whole Client Model will also affect the wealthy client's perception of your character (a rating of 7.2).

Exhibit 9.3 | The Potential Impact of Using The Whole Client Model

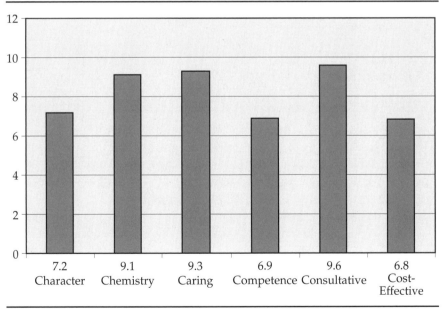

N = 1,417 Middle-Class Millionaires

Practice Implications

Central to the success of the wealth management process is to have an in-depth understanding of affluent clients. Most financial advisors stumble because they are unable to develop the requisite in-depth profile. As a methodology for profiling the wealthy, the Whole Client Model fits the bill perfectly. In the trenches, the Whole Client Model is credited with being the catalyst in creating loyal wealthy clients who, in turn, become advocates of the wealth manager. This results in a steady stream of high-quality affluent referrals (see *Chapter 12: Generating Middle-Class Millionaire Client Referrals*). Moreover, the Whole Client Model has been proven in expanding strategic partnerships with other advisors, resulting in a steady stream of new HNW referrals from these advisors (see *Chapter 13: Creating a Pipeline of New Middle-Class Millionaire Clients from Accountants and Attorneys*).

While most financial advisors have some trouble, at first, in mastering the Whole Client Model, effort and practice, persistence and sometimes a little coaching is all that is required for the majority of financial advisors to become quite adept with the methodology. And, with experience, financial advisors make the Whole Client Model their own, developing their core list of questions, as well as a comfort level with how to ask the questions and follow-up.

For your consideration:

- *How similar is the Whole Client Model to the way you're doing fact-finding today?*
- *Where are the significant differences?*
- *Which categories of the Whole Client Model are you proficient in today?*
- *Which categories are new to you?*

Exercise #1 | Working the Whole Client Model

1. Let's begin with the ten middle-class millionaires you have been using in the previous exercises. Using the questions we detailed above and employing the Whole Client Model graphic, profile each one of them.
2. What information is missing for each profile?
3. How do you plan to fill in the blanks?
4. Specify the additional opportunities that exist for you to provide additional investment management products and services, as well as the opportunities to provide non-investment management products and services.

If you are like most financial advisors, there are a number of blanks in your profiles. If this is the case, do not let it slow you down. As we have said previously, this is common. It takes a lot of time and work to become truly expert with this process. However, by using the Whole Client Model, you are taking the first and essential step to being able to efficaciously provide additional financial products and services—the crucial step to becoming a wealth manager.

Exercise #2 | **Into the Field**

5. Identify 10 to 20 new affluent clients from your book—wealthy clients you have done some business with but you feel there is much more that you can and want to do.
6. Set up appointments with them.
7. Profile them using the Whole Client Model.
8. Identify additional business opportunities.
9. Go to each meeting and make sure you end each meeting with very concrete "next steps" and a timetable.

One of the best ways to learn a skill, any skill, is, of course, by practicing it. Even if you do not feel you have mastered the Whole Client Model completely, the most effective way to do so is by using it with real affluent clients. In all probability, you are doing a great many things right. So, it is time to go into the field and better serve your affluent clients—and profit as well.

YOUR WEALTH MANAGEMENT TEAM

- *In the financial advisory business—broadly defined—what do you do exceptionally well?*
- *What are your professional limitations?*
- *How are you dealing with your professional limitations today?*
- *What is a wealth management team?*
- *Why do you need to have one?*

The rewards for investment-oriented financial advisors who transition to a wealth management orientation are significant. From more loyal, affluent clients to being able to find wealthier clients, wealth managers are, for the majority of financial advisors, the preferred practice model. Furthermore, financial advisors who make the transition can increase their incomes by 35 percent or more within a year.

Wealth management is all about delivering solutions predicated on financial products and services to affluent clients in a consultative manner. By employing the Whole Client Model, you are able to develop a comprehensive profile of a middle-class millionaire client. With these insights in hand, you are positioned to deliver the appropriate solution.

The complication is that the best solution may very well not be within your sphere of expertise. We have found, with tremendous regularity, that most financial advisors have no experience in the "solutions" required by their clients—hence the necessity for a wealth management team, a network of specialists.

Middle-class millionaires do not expect you to be an expert in everything. In fact, you can create more loyal, affluent clients by being able to bring in the appropriate experts (Exhibit 10.1). Two-thirds of loyal, affluent clients (66.8 percent) note that their primary financial advisor has a wealth management team available. Only two-fifths of the satisfied, affluent clients (40.1 percent) say the same thing. Meanwhile, 29.8 percent of moderately satisfied, affluent clients say their primary financial advisor has a wealth management team available.

Exhibit 10.1 | Their Primary Financial Advisor Brings The Appropriate Experts Into The Process

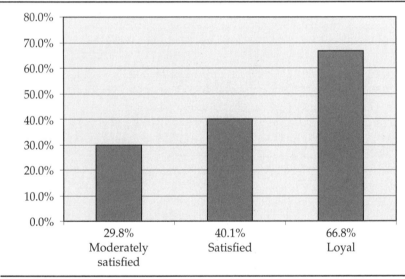

N = 1,417 Middle-Class Millionaires

Wealth managers are able to develop an in-depth understanding of an affluent client and provide a wide array of potential solutions. As we noted, the ability for an individual to be adept at the spectrum of possible solutions is exceedingly rare. Consequently, to be a successful wealth manager, you must put together a network of specialists that can be called on when appropriate.

Teamwork takes work. Establishing and maintaining a network of specialists is not an easy task. Let's examine what it takes to build and keep up such a network. There are four phases in this process. They are:

- Phase I: Deciding on the Required Specialists

- Phase II: Locating the Desired Specialists
- Phase III: Building the Team
- Phase IV: Managing the Team

Phase I | Deciding on the Required Specialists

Because of the time and effort required to develop and maintain a smooth running, prosperous wealth management team, it behooves you to be as economical in your efforts as possible. Therefore, you need to start by deciding what expertise you do not have but require in order to excel.

The way to start is by clearly delineating you own area(s) of specialization. It might be in the field of fee-based money management or more narrowly in portfolio construction or not in the investment management business at all. Your expertise might be in managing the expectations of the affluent. You need to be very honest with yourself and specify what you are particularly good at.

After looking inside, it is time to look outside. Based on your current clientele, what are the most prevalent and important financial issues and problems they are facing. These are the issues you will need to address and problems you will need to solve. And, if you do not have the expertise yourself, you will certainly need to tap someone who does.

If you work extensively with corporate executives, for example, you will likely need a hedging specialist. If you work with many affluent physicians, then an asset protection-planning specialist is in order.

If your "ideal client" is the middle-class millionaire, then knowing their key concerns (see *Chapter 2: Key Concerns of Middle-Class Millionaires*), as well as being familiar with their use of financial products and services (see *Chapter 3: Financial Products and Services*) will provide you with insights that can, at least initially, expedite your determination of the required specialists.

You should not get caught up in deciding on the required specialists to the point where it slows you down from working with affluent clients. We have seen far too many financial advisors unable to get out of their own way because they got so wrapped up in Phase I. Whatever collection of specialists you decide on today will very likely have to be modified as your wealth management practice evolves. So, the lesson is to take your best shot, realizing that the specialists you will need will always be a work in progress.

Phase II | Locating the Desired Specialists

If you are part of a larger financial institution, such as a bank or brokerage firm, the requisite specialists might be employees of the firm. So, if a hedging specialist is required, he or she might be just a phone call away in another department at the financial institution. Some of the financial institutions have established arrangements with outside specialists, such as attorneys, to facilitate the ability of their financial advisors to provide services not done in-house (such as estate planning).

In the majority of situations, this works out quite well for the financial advisors on the road to becoming a wealth manager. The working arrangements of the specialist within the financial institution are already set. On the other hand, it is not uncommon for these specialists:

- to be impossible to get a hold of when their expertise is required;
- are not really good enough considering the nature of the client;
- are unable to be good team participants.

In these situations, when it is possible—such as when the financial institution does not require using their in-house experts—the wealth manager will need to look outside the firm for specialists. While many aspiring wealth managers initially feel finding the desired specialists is a daunting task, experience shows us it is not that hard once financial advisors start looking. You can find specialists online, by word-of-mouth, by reading trade magazines, even by your affluent clients themselves. However you do it, just build a list of possible desired specialists.

Often a professional you might know—an accountant, say—will know some of the better private client lawyers. Similarly, if there are in-house experts, they will know who the top people in related fields are that are not employed at the firm.

In effect, through classic networking you can identify the specialists you will need as part of your wealth management team. Interestingly, we have observed that once wealth managers have found a couple of requisite specialists, they are easily able to find the other specialists they might need. For example, after finding a leading authority on the use of life insurance in advanced estate planning, a wealth manager learns who the other talented life insurance consultants, as well as the leading trusts and estates lawyers are in his or her area; in effect, who all the other potential specialists are with this expertise for his or her network.

This growing awareness has led to another way of locating the desired specialists for budding wealth managers. They are turning to the more seasoned wealth managers for recommendations on who they should approach to be part of their network. And, with many specialists being experts on specific services or transactions, we are seeing a number of wealth managers employing the same experts.

Phase III | Building the Team

Every potential specialist must meet the following four criteria:

- *Specific expertise.* Possessing "unique" knowledge and talents is the first screen in selecting a specialist. The expertise in question must also complement your competencies and skills without being redundant. This is precisely what you will accomplish in locating the desired specialist. Still, you must be sensitive to the limitations of the specialist.
- *Integrity.* The highest ethical standards are indispensable, of course. You must know where the specialist draws the line in the sand. In other words, what types of transactions, for instance, will the specialist not execute.
- *Professionalism.* In every way from responsiveness to inquiries to perpetual learning to affluent client management, the network of participants must embrace professionalism.
- *Chemistry between you and the specialist.* There needs to be a comfort level when it comes to working with each of your network participants. All of the expert knowledge in the world is valueless if there is no rapport between you and your specialists.

Your network of specialists must work as a team, even if it is only a team of two—you and an individual specialist. And, central to this team running well is for everyone to clearly understand who is leading the team. And that person is you—the wealth manager.

Phase IV | Managing the Team

Once a high-quality network is put in place, it is up to you to maintain and manage it. You will also have to spell out financial arrangements, presuming the financial arrangements are not already set because the specialists are coming through existing arrangements established by the financial institution.

There are three popular types of financial arrangements in the wealth management business. The first is fee-for-service through which the wealth manager buys—or rents—expertise on a case-by-case basis. With a retainer arrangement, the specialist is paid a monthly or annual fee so that they are available for consultations, usually by phone. Finally, some specialists are on a retainer and also get compensated by fee-for-service. Interestingly, what tends to "blow up" a wealth management team is usually not related to the financial arrangements, but is a function of the egos of the specialists.

There are two types of "bad behaviors" specialists can engage in. One is excessive independence. You never—never, ever—hand an affluent client off to a specialist. The specialist is a "utility" being brought in for a very specific purpose. The specialist should never contact the client without your permission. We strongly recommend that you be at every meeting between the middle-class millionaire client and the specialist unless the affluent client wants it otherwise.

The other act of bad behavior is referred to as "intellect run amok." You are choosing specialists who are very smart. The problem is that some of these very smart people cannot help themselves and like to show off (they may not even know they are doing it). In these situations, the specialists are so involved in preening that they can derail the process and upend business getting done.

If a specialist engages in these "bad behaviors," you should fire him or her from the team. It is essential for all the team participants to always be aware of who is leading the team. Who is calling the shots? That is you—the wealth manager.

Strategic Scenario Sessions

You are not expert at everything, so you need a wealth management team. However, a pervasive mistake made by many financial advisors is not leveraging the expertise of the specialists from the start.

For example, there are many ways to manage a concentrated stock position (from selling the stock to hedging the position, and from private annuities to charitable entities). Let's say you are not familiar with all of them, but on your team is a hedging specialist and a high-quality private client lawyer. By reviewing with them the situation, they will discuss with you the techniques they are familiar with to address the matter. Then, based on your more intimate knowledge of the middle-class millionaire client, you can decide the best course of action.

The point is that by bringing your specialists into discussions surrounding each of your affluent clients, you will:

- find additional solutions for your wealthy clients;
- learn more about your clients and the opportunities they represent enabling you to more readily spot them with other affluent clients;
- enhance the cohesiveness of your wealth management team through participation and by enabling the specialists to see where they can profit.

Operationally, you take the information you collected from a middle-class millionaire client by using the Whole Client Model and present it to your specialists. Optimally, everyone would be in the same room at the time. However, often not all the members of your wealth management team are required. And, it is not uncommon to do this by phone.

You and your wealth management team or selected team members need to brainstorm about the affluent client. We refer to these brainstorming get-togethers as *strategic scenario sessions*. In the end, you will likely come up with any or all of the following:

- more questions you need answered;
- a number of potential solutions to the affluent client's situation;
- the ability to walk the middle-class millionaire through a few high-probability scenarios;
- knowledge of how to facilitate the implementation of possible scenarios; and
- an understating of what is going to be required to keep everything moving forward.

Interestingly, when it comes to middle-class millionaires and their concerns (see *Chapter 2: Key Concerns of Middle-Class Millionaires*), by running a number of strategic scenario sessions, you will quickly become adept at the array of high-probability scenarios. We are not saying that you will become an expert—be as knowledgeable and capable as the specialists you are using—but you will be able to recognize fact patterns and their implications in real time. And, all this helps in creating loyal clients—especially when it comes to being perceived as competent as well as being consultative.

Practice Implications

It can take a considerable amount of time and effort to establish and maintain a network of specialists—your wealth management team. However, once you have your specialists in place and have developed the appropriate working relationship, the network tends to run smoothly. So, if a top-of-the-line private client lawyer is one of the specialists, once he or she has been recruited to the network and understands how to be a good team player, the energies it takes to manage that person becomes minimal. The same can be said about all the specialists you make part of your wealth management team.

Another way to gauge if your team is worth the effort is to consider the options. Without a network of specialists, a financial advisor is unable to transition into a wealth manager. So if the decision is to be a wealth manager and garner all the accompanying practice and financial benefits, there really is not much of a choice.

Leveraging your wealth management team from the beginning by conducting *strategic scenario sessions* will enable you to get your wealth management practice moving into high gear quickly. *Strategic scenario sessions* will also provide you with the "real life" education you need to be able to very effectively identify opportunities with your middle-class millionaire clients in "real time."

A few questions:

- *What are the ways to manage a concentrated stock position?*
- *Who would you need on your wealth management team if this were a service you needed to provide your middle-class millionaire clients?*
- *What are the ways of freezing the value of real assets in an estate?*
- *Who would you need on your wealth management team if this were a service you needed to provide your middle-class millionaire clients?*

Exercise #1 | Determining Your Expertise and Your Specialists

1. Write down a list of critical success factors for your wealth management practice with middle-class millionaires.
2. Next to each critical success factor put a number from 1 (not at all expert) to 10 (extremely expert).
3. Make two lists. One list should be composed of the critical success factors you rated 9 or 10. The other list is the rest of the critical success factors.
4. Next to each of the critical success factors on your list that you did not rate a 9 or a 10, write down the *type* of specialist you will require.

When we conduct this exercise with financial advisors, they tend to become anxious as they realize that there are so many critical success factors where they are not particularly strong. When this happens, we know we are getting honest answers. Moreover, it shows the financial advisors the challenges to becoming wealth managers. We have yet to run into a financial advisor who, with some coaching, has not been able to smooth out those challenges.

Exercise #2 | Conducting *Strategic Scenario Sessions*

1. For your ten middle-class millionaires, take the data you collected and conduct a strategic scenario session for each of them.
2. Which specialists should participate in the strategic scenario session?
3. Detail the possible solutions for each affluent client.
4. Determine the benefits to your practice, as well as to the specialists for each scenario.

The best way to become a top-of-the-line wealth manager is not by taking classes on technical fields where a little knowledge will make you dangerous or by attending workshops on what and how to do wealth management. On the contrary, the best and quickest way to make that transition to becoming a wealth manager is by practicing where it counts—with affluent clients. So, go to work.

KEY LESSONS

Wealth management is the consultative process of meeting the needs and wants of affluent clients by providing the appropriate financial products and services. Wealth management entails coordinating a team of specialists to address the needs and wants of affluent clients.

For the greater majority of financial advisors, wealth management is the solution. Wealth management will enable you to:

- better serve your middle-class millionaire clients by addressing their needs and wants as opposed to "pushing product;"
- create more loyal affluent clients with all the accompanying benefits to your practice for doing so;
- work with fewer but wealthier affluent clients;
- create a larger pool of investable assets for you to manage;
- increase your income by 35 percent or more starting in the first year.

There are two key principals to building a highly successful wealth management practice. The first is the Whole Client Model. It is one of the best ways of collecting and organizing client data. By using the Whole Client Model, you will be able to get a broader and deeper understanding of each of your affluent clients; also, you will be able to see the inter-relationships among the various facts and categories. This in turn, sets the stage for you to provide viable and highly attractive solutions to your wealthy clients.

For many financial advisors, the Whole Client Model can be daunting at first. However, with time and persistence, we have found that it can become second nature—almost instinctive—for financial advisors. We have provided you with a battery of questions for each category of the Whole Client Model. By employing the methodology, you will find those questions that work for you. Furthermore, you will make the process of asking the questions your own, taking advantage of your individual personality and style.

The best way to become adept with the Whole Client Model is to use it. Practice, practice, practice. It is the only way.

The second principal key to building a highly successful wealth management practice is putting together your wealth management team. It is impossible for you to be expert at everything and your affluent clients would probably run for the hills if you insisted that you were. On the contrary, your middle-class millionaire clients want to work with experts and are more than happy for you to coordinate the specialists on their behalf.

In practice, the most difficult part of building and maintaining your wealth management team is keeping all the specialists focused, and ensuring that you are in the driver's seat. The very nature of the experts you will end up calling on, necessitates astute management—from sharing a compelling vision to making certain no one goes brain dead, and making sure everyone gets compensated appropriately.

The combination of the Whole Client Model and your network of specialists can and should result in *strategic scenario sessions*. These are brainstorming opportunities that enable you to identify and position "solutions" for your affluent clients, as well as provide you an education on the various "solutions" to different fact patterns.

In the exercises we asked you to do, once again, concentrate on the same ten middle-class millionaires you have been considering since the beginning of the book. You should be able to see how to help them (as well as your own practice) by adopting the wealth management perspective. Now, you need to put what we have been detailing into action. Go out and see them.

What we have concentrated on is your ability to capitalize on your existing middle-class millionaire clientele. This can translate into a minimum of a 35 percent increase in your income within the first year. However, at some point you are going to need new blood—new wealthy clients. In the next section, we provide you with the insights, methodologies, tools and tactics to cultivate new middle-class millionaires.

PART
4

FINDING
MIDDLE-CLASS
MILLIONAIRES

FOCUS ON REFERRALS

- *What are all the ways of finding middle-class millionaires?*
- *What approaches do you use most often?*
- *Which prospecting strategy resulted in your acquiring your ten wealthy clients?*
- *Which prospecting strategy has resulted in acquiring your wealthiest client?*

There are a wide variety of prospecting approaches—client referrals, seminars, cold calling and public relations activities. Every one of them can make it possible for you to acquire new affluent clients. Most financial advisors employ a mix of prospecting strategies. Still, the key is to concentrate your efforts on those prospecting strategies that will result in the most cost-effective results.

In our research study, we found that HNW clients prefer to find their primary financial advisors by referrals (Exhibit 11.1). First in importance are referrals from the other professional advisors they employ, such as accountants and attorneys (54.2 percent). Second is a referral from another client of the financial advisor (30.1 percent).

Exhibit 11.1 | Importance in Finding Their Primary Financial Advisor

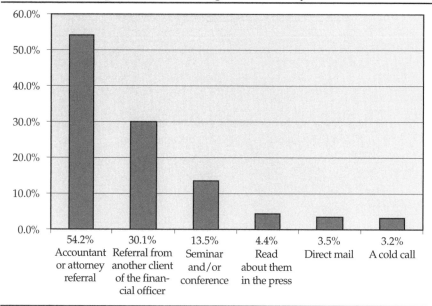

| 54.2%
Accountant
or attorney
referral | 30.1%
Referral from
another client
of the finan-
cial officer | 13.5%
Seminar
and/or
conference | 4.4%
Read
about them
in the press | 3.5%
Direct mail | 3.2%
A cold call |

N = 1,417 Middle-Class Millionaires

Exhibit 11.2 | Perceived Value of Prospecting Strategies

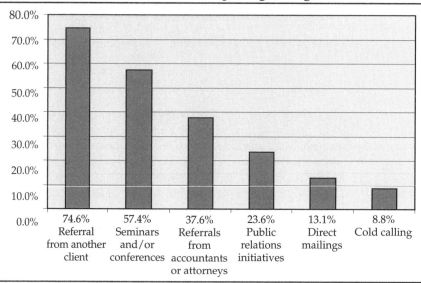

| 74.6%
Referral
from another
client | 57.4%
Seminars
and/or
conferences | 37.6%
Referrals
from
accountants
or attorneys | 23.6%
Public
relations
initiatives | 13.1%
Direct
mailings | 8.8%
Cold calling |

N = 512 Financial Advisors

Turning to the 512 financial advisors we surveyed, we find that client referrals is considered the number one prospecting strategy [74.6 percent (Exhibit 11.2)]. This is followed by seminars and conferences (57.4 percent). Then we have accountant or attorney referrals (37.6 percent).

As we will see below, accountant and attorney referrals are critical to building a significant financial advisory practice with middle-class millionaires. Yet the average advisor isn't good at acquiring middle-class millionaire clients from accountants and attorneys. Hence, we will provide you with a systematic methodology to do so (see *Chapter 13: Creating a Pipeline of New Middle-Class Millionaire Clients from Accountants and Attorneys*).

As we said, any prospecting approach can be effective. However, referrals from your affluent clients or from accountants and attorneys are best. That's because middle-class millionaires prefer to find their high-quality financial advisors by referral from trusted sources.

The Logic of Referrals

The logic of referrals is supported by three considerations:

- *The intangibility of the financial product and services offered.* From the affluent client's point of view, financial products and services are something of a mystery. The services a financial advisor provides cannot be seen or touched or evaluated directly. Research shows that when a service is important, and intangible, people will try to reduce their risk of making a bad choice by asking other people's opinion.
- *The perceived complexity of the financial services offered.* Wealthy clients believe that their situation is important, unique and complicated. As a result, they invest considerable time and effort searching for a financial advisor who is just right for them.
- *The desire on the part of middle-class millionaires to work with "authorities" coupled with a general inability to identify the "authorities."* Since the wealthy believe that their situations are complex, they want an expert—a true authority—to work on their case. The best way to find out if a financial advisor is an authority on the unique problems of the wealthy is to get the opinions of other wealthy people or other authorities.

Looking at the situation through the eyes of the affluent, we can easily see the importance of referrals. When a wealthy person comes to believe they need a new financial advisor, they ask around and get a referral. The reason they do so is because they cannot personally compare the work of one financial advisor to another (intangibility), they think their situation is unique (complexity) and they want the best (reliance on authorities). The implication is clear. If wealthy clients are finding financial advisors via referrals, you need to get into the position of being on the receiving end of these referrals.

Affluent Client Referrals Compared
to Accountant and Attorney Referrals

What we want to make perfectly clear is that you need to concentrate your efforts on both types of referrals—those from your affluent clients and those from other professional advisors, such as accountants and attorneys. When it comes to sourcing new middle-class millionaires, both approaches will bear fruit, so both approaches should be actively pursued.

What we have seen in previous research is that financial advisors tend to make a much more concerted effort at obtaining referrals from their affluent clients then they do from the likes of accountants and attorneys; the problem is that even these efforts are not good enough. While it is essential to make every effort to garner affluent client referrals from your clients, you will need to create strategic partnerships with a select few "centers of influence."

The simple fact is that the greater the clients' wealth, the more inclined they are to follow the recommendations of their accountants and attorneys (Exhibit 11.3). For those affluent clients with a net-worth between $1 million and $3 million, referrals from their peers are more important than referrals from accountants and attorneys (41.8 percent compared to 30.1 percent). On the other hand, when we look at middle-class millionaires with net-worths of $3 million to $10 million, accountant or attorney referrals dominate (82.4 percent compared to 16.4 percent).

Exhibit 11.3 | Importance in Finding Their
Primary Financial Advisor by Net-Worth

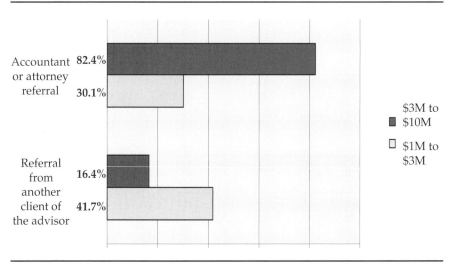

N = 1,417 Middle-Class Millionaires

We asked financial advisors: "In the last 12 months, how did you get your best new affluent client (investable assets of $500,000 or more)?" And we found that referrals from accountants and attorneys rule [64.4 percent (Exhibit 11.4)]. For 29.5 percent of the financial advisors, their best, new affluent client came from a referral from a current client. And, 6.1 percent of the financial advisors sourced their best, new affluent client some other way, such as a seminar—or the wealthy client came in over the transom.

Exhibit 11.4 | Sourcing Their Best, New Affluent Client

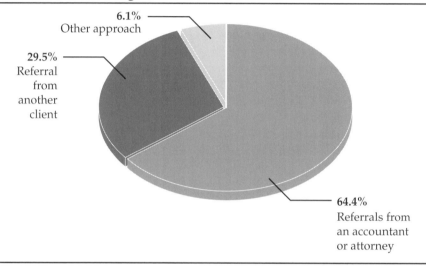

N = 512 Financial Advisors

It is no secret that referrals from accountants and attorneys have always been a powerful way to win new affluent clients. Indeed, referrals from accountants and attorneys are much more powerful than affluent client referrals. By examining the two prospecting approaches side-by-side we can see why (Exhibit 11.5).

Exhibit 11.5 | Client Referrals Compared to Professional Referrals

Factors	Client Referrals	Professional Referrals
Number of potential referrals	Relatively few	Potentially extensive
Opportunity to refer	Limited	Pervasive
Extent of prequalification	Low to Moderate	High
Likelihood of accepting the referral	Low to Moderate	Moderate to High

Source: Creating a Pipeline of New Affluent Clients (2003)

Your middle-class millionaire clients will tend to know relatively few other qualified potential affluent clients. On the other hand, think of how many affluent clients a lawyer or an accountant has. Middle-class millionaires have a limited opportunity to make a referral, as financial and related topics do not come up in everyday conversation. In contrast, it is the job of lawyers and accountants to be on the lookout for issues that their wealthy clients need resolved and for the experts whose knowledge and skills are necessary. Accountants and lawyers, by the nature of their contract with their wealthy clients, can introduce you and the work you do into the conversation whenever it is appropriate. Given the situation most of their affluent clients are in, there is almost always an appropriate time.

Compared to your current affluent clients, middle-class millionaires tend to only have a vague idea of the net worth and/or investable assets of their wealthy peers. Accountants and lawyers, in comparison, have extensive knowledge of their affluent clients' financials, making it much easier to ensure that the wealthy clients they refer you to are indeed wealthy, as well as interested in speaking with you.

And when accountants and attorneys refer wealthy clients, there is a very good chance those referrals will turn into new affluent clients for financial advisors. The same cannot be said for referrals you receive from your current middle-class millionaire clientele.

What does this all mean? Affluent client referrals are, and will remain, an important way for you to garner more wealthy clients. It is a prospecting strategy that you should implement ardently, and we provide a systematic process to do so (see *Chapter 12: Generating Middle-Class Millionaire Client Referrals*).

Affluent client referrals from accountants and attorneys are the best way to prospect. Therefore, if you are not making this prospecting approach a central part of your prospecting efforts, you are letting the best opportunity slip by. In *Chapter 13: Creating a Pipeline of New Middle-Class Millionaire Clients from Accountants and Attorneys*, we detail the conceptual basis and the systematic methodology for creating a steady stream of new, highly-qualified affluent client referrals from these professionals.

Practice Implications

Referrals to new middle-class millionaires are essential to building a strong practice predicated on affluent clients. Your referrals should come from your existing clients as well as "centers of influence"—accountants and attorneys. We are not saying that you should concentrate exclusively upon referrals, but rather it should be one important prospecting tool. You should always remember how important referrals are to middle-class millionaires because of the intangibility and complexity of financial products and services, as well as the desire on the part of affluent clients to work with "authorities."

The complication is that relatively few financial advisors are particularly adept in sourcing new middle-class millionaire clients from accountants and attorneys—a conundrum we will assist in rectifying. What is most important is to employ both approaches to sourcing new affluent clients. Referrals are key from whatever the source.

For your consideration:

- *Within the last year, how did you obtain the majority of your new wealthy clients?*
- *What about your best affluent client?*
- *What are you doing to replicate these results?*
- *How systematic are you in asking for referrals from your clients or from "centers of influence"?*
- *What obstacles are in your way?*

Exercise #1 | Sourcing New Middle-Class Millionaire Clients

1. How many new affluent clients did you win in the last 12 months?
2. How did they end up talking to you?
3. Describe what steps, if any, you took to source more middle-class millionaire clients.
4. What do you need to do to source more middle-class millionaire clients today?

If you are like the majority of financial advisors, referrals—probably from your current clientele—are your most effective way to garner new affluent clients. Also, if you are like the majority of financial advisors, you are not being very systematic in the way you are getting these affluent client referrals.

Exercise #2 | The Importance of Referrals

5. Take a piece if paper and divide it in two.
6. On one side write down Client Referrals. On the other side write down "Centers of Influence" Referrals.
7. Why it is so essential to the ultimate success in growing your practice profitably?
8. On another piece of paper identify the issues you have in getting these types of referrals.

Generally, we find that financial advisors understand the central role of referrals to building a business. What also proves to be very informative is the list of hurdles financial advisors have in obtaining referrals. In all probability, many of your issues will vanish as you employ the methodologies we will now be discussing.

GENERATING MIDDLE-CLASS MILLIONAIRE CLIENT REFERRALS

- *Before you will be able to obtain referrals to middle-class millionaires from other middle-class millionaires, what will you need to do?*
- *What obstacles are in your way?*
- *What is the role of high-net-worth psychological profiles in obtaining affluent client referrals?*
- *What is the role of the Whole Client Model?*

Very few financial advisors focusing on middle-class millionaires do not recognize the value of getting client referrals. At the same time, we find that relatively few financial advisors get as many referrals from their own clients as they would like. There are a number of reasons for this; amazingly, more than half of the financial advisors (56.8 percent) fail to regularly ask their client for referrals (Exhibit 12.1).

Exhibit 12.1 | Financial Advisors Who, in The Last Six Months, Asked Their Affluent Clients For a Referral

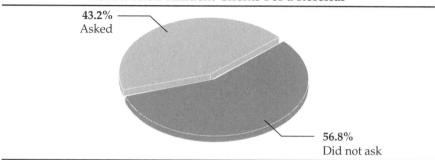

43.2%
Asked

56.8%
Did not ask

N = 512 Financial Advisors

One problem is that most financial advisors do not know how to ask—or even whom to ask. You have to create a systematic process for asking. This brings us back to the nine high-net-worth personalities of middle-class millionaires.

The Role of High-Net-Worth Psychology to Obtain Affluent Client Referrals

Different high-net-worth personalities have different attitudes toward making referrals. Some types of affluent clients have large networks they can plug you into, and other high-net-worth personalities have smaller networks, or none as in the case of the Anonymous. Furthermore, the different high-net-worth personalities have different tendencies when making referrals (Exhibit 12.2).

Exhibit 12.2 | The Role of High-Net-Worth Psychology in Sourcing New Affluent Clients

High-Net-Worth Personality	Social Ties	Willingness to Refer
Family Stewards	Strong	High
VIPs	Strong	Medium
Moguls	Strong	Medium
Independents	Medium	High
Gamblers	Medium	High
Innovators	Medium	High
Accumulators	Medium	Medium
Phobics	Medium	Low
The Anonymous	Low	Low

Source: High-Net-Worth Psychology (1999)

Family Stewards are great for client referral development. They tend to be well connected in their communities and have extensive social networks. Additionally, Family Stewards are generally quite willing to provide referrals of their friends and business associates, since they are often helpful by nature.

VIPs are also well connected. However, VIPs are well connected because of the status they seek among their peers. They like knowing important people and like being thought of as important. VIPs are somewhat more lukewarm to the idea of referrals, although they would be willing to make referrals if they can see how their own prestige would be enhanced.

Moguls, given their drive for control, have strong personal and professional networks as an extension of their influence and power. They are less likely to leverage their networks on your behalf unless there is some way they can also benefit. If they can sense they will gain an advantage if they introduce you to someone, they will do so. Thus, you would need to create a clearly defined win-win scenario to motivate Moguls to procure new affluent clients for you.

Independents have networks that tend to center around their hobbies or avocations. They will know people who are committed to the same personal goals as they are and, under the proper circumstances, will readily make introductions for you.

Gamblers have networks that share their obsession with the stock market and investing. Because of their involvement with investing, gamblers can be highly motivated to refer you to others who share these same interests.

Innovators are generally pretty solitary people. Because of their likely technical backgrounds, they will tend to know other people with a similar orientation. At the same time, Innovators can be extremely enthusiastic about investing and will, when properly motivated, refer people to you.

Accumulators are a diverse group, so it is hard to typify the people in their networks except that they generally have more modest life styles, relatively speaking. Accumulators are willing to refer people to you, but this is predicated on your ability to deliver meaningful investment returns to them. You would be well advised only to make your requests for referrals at times when you deliver excellent portfolio performance.

Phobics have a relatively small network that tends to consist of close friends, family and key business associates. However, while many of these people might indeed be middle-class millionaires, the likelihood is low that they will refer you to people in their social or professional networks.

The Anonymous are extremely close-mouthed about financial matters. They often have a more limited social network than the other high-net-worth personalities. They are most likely not going to refer anyone to you, as it would be a violation of that person's privacy. The best policy is not to ask for referrals of the Anonymous for it will only hurt your relationship with them.

Knowing the high-net-worth personalities of your middle-class million-aires will certainly enable you to put the odds of getting affluent client refer-rals in your favor. Still, it is imperative to employ a systematic process to generate new wealthy client referrals.

How to Generate Affluent Client Referrals

Once in a while, a middle-class millionaire will provide you with an un-solicited affluent client referral. However, why would you depend on such a dicey prospecting strategy when you can create a stream of wealthy client referrals by being systematic and proactive?

For the most part, when your loyal clients are asked (and asked in the proper manner), they will come through with affluent client referrals. The process for soliciting client referrals is made up of seven steps. There are no great secrets for obtaining client referrals. As always, the key is consistency.

You should think of these seven steps as an outline that you will adapt based on your own working style and preferences. Your personality and working style will make the methodology unique to you. As you become more skilled at obtaining affluent client referrals, you should continue to modify the seven-step methodology to create a personal approach that works best for you.

The seven steps are:

- Step #1: Set expectations
- Step #2: Create loyal clients
- Step #3: Focus on previously identified affluent prospects
- Step #4: Ask for the referral
- Step #5: Say "Thank you"
- Step #6: Inform your affluent client how the meeting went
- Step #7: Say "Thank you" again

Let's now drill down on each of the steps.

Step #1: Set expectations. Optimally, you want to create the appropriate set of client expectations from the beginning of every relationship. From the start, explain to your affluent clients how you will be checking in frequently to gauge their satisfaction with what is going on and, very importantly, to uncover any problems before they metastasize.

And, early on in your relationship with wealthy clients let them know you appreciate referrals.

Step #2: Create loyal, affluent clients. In *Chapter 4: The Value of Loyalty*, we saw that loyal middle-class millionaire clients produced 11.8 qualified affluent referrals in the previous 12 months. This is about six times more than a satisfied affluent client would provide.

We also saw that 81.6 percent of loyal middle-class millionaires are "very" or "extremely" likely to make referrals to their primary financial advisor within the forthcoming year. Meanwhile, the likelihood of satisfied and moderately satisfied, affluent clients making referrals to their primary advisor in the next year is negligible.

Step #3: Identify wealthy prospects. If you were to ask a wealthy client if they knew anyone who could use your expertise, you would often find that your clients do not know anyone at all. We know this is not the case, but the "do-you-know-someone" question is usually planted in barren ground.

Your chances of getting an affluent client referral is exponentially greater when you talk about people the middle-class millionaire knows you would like to meet. Therefore, it behooves you to have predetermined whom the wealthy client knows. Then you can be specific when you ask for referrals.

How do you find out who those people are? The answer is when you are learning about your affluent client using the Whole Client Model. For example, let's say your wealthy client owns a business that makes furniture. When you are talking about his or her professional relationships, you need to identify all the other businesses and their owners he or she works with, such as the shipping company and the material suppliers. At a later date, you can use this information to set the stage to ask about specific people you would like to be introduced to.

Step #4: Ask for the referral. Frankly, it is rare for wealthy clients to wake up one morning and think about providing affluent referrals to their financial advisors. You have to take the initiative if you want the referral.

There are many different variations, but here is the general game plan. Talk about the benefits of your services; talk about how progress has been made toward the affluent client's goals; and, remember to speak to them in the context of his or her high-net-worth personality. Wealthy clients tend to know other wealthy clients with the same high-net-worth personality. Then you can tie this part of the conversation to specific individuals you want to meet—via Step #3.

Step #5: Say: "Thank you." You must recognize there is a social and personal cost to your middle-class millionaire clients for providing you with referrals. Because of this cost, you should quickly reciprocate and show gratitude. Moreover, thanking your affluent clients for referrals provides you with another opportunity to maintain contact. At the same time, you are also given the opportunity to reinforce your relationships with your clients.

Step #6: Inform your affluent client how the meeting went. Your affluent client will be curious as to how things went. It is important that you let him or her know that things went well, but be mindful of confidentiality.

One of the first things your referring affluent client will want to know is whether or not you were able to make contact with the person. He or she will also want to be reassured that the initial meeting went well. One way to provide your wealthy client feedback is with a quick note or email. Notes and emails can be better than phone calls because they do not have to be returned and no one wants to play phone tag. Of course, you will want to make some of these follow-up contacts over the phone to explore whether any new needs or wants have arisen, as well as to build on your existing relationships.

It is important to protect the confidentiality of the affluent prospect. Never disclose personal information or the business of one client to another.

Step #7: Say "Thank you" again. Just because you thanked your client for the referral once, do not stop there. Thank him or her again. Especially thank him or her if you close some business.

Practice Implications

Unless clients are loyal to you, you will not receive many referrals. Therefore, creating loyal clients is a must. You also have to ask for what you want, and, of course, what you want are referrals to middle-class millionaires. We saw that many financial advisors are not asking.

The seven-step process will help you generate a constant stream of wealthy clients by leveraging your existing clientele. Keep in mind that high-net-worth psychological profiles will help you in this process as it will help you anticipate who else your clients know (who is in their social and professional networks) and how to ask for referrals (and who not to approach).

A few questions:

- *Are you asking for referrals from your clients on a regular basis?*
- *If not, why not?*
- *Are you asking for referrals or for specific referrals?*
- *Are you aware of the middle-class millionaires your clients can refer you to?*

Exercise #1 | Issues in Asking for Affluent Client Referrals

1. Calculate the number of middle-class millionaire client referrals you received in the previous 12 months from your current clients.
2. How did you get each of those referrals?
3. On a scale of 1 (not at all systematic) to 10 (extremely systematic), rank how systematic you were in obtaining the referral.

We have found that, by and large, financial advisors are not very systematic in sourcing new affluent clients from their current clients. When financial advisors do get such referrals, they have tended to be erratic and sometimes they do not even know how they came about. To build a highly successful financial advisory practice with affluent clients, you need to be consistently doing what it takes to generate affluent client referrals.

Exercise #2 | Identifying Affluent Prospects

1. Returning to your list of 10 middle-class millionaires, write down 3 to 5 people of wealth they know socially.
2. Now, write down 3 to 5 affluent people they know professionally.
3. For each of these 10 prospects, write down the way you will motivate your middle-class millionaire clients to introduce you to them.

We know that by prompting a wealthy client to a specific colleague or friend, you are exponentially more likely to get the referral. However, this approach is alien to a great many financial advisors. Use the Whole Client Model (or any other process, for that matter) that will enable you to discern who your wealthy client knows.

CREATING A PIPELINE OF NEW MIDDLE-CLASS MILLIONAIRE CLIENTS FROM ACCOUNTANTS AND ATTORNEYS

- *How many "strong relationships" do you have with lawyers and accountants?*
- *What is your definition of a "strong relationship"?*
- *What are you doing to build "strong relationships" with accountants and attorneys?*
- *What is THE most important thing you need to know about a trusts and estates lawyer you are seeking referrals from?*
- *What is the second most important thing you need to know?*
- *What is the third?*

There is a lot of competition for middle-class millionaires. You are not the first (and you will not be the last) to follow the logical path to get to this point. When you consider the data and listen to the stories of how financial advisors found many of their wealthier clients, it all comes down to generating referrals from professionals, such as accountants and attorneys.

The senior executives of quite a number of financial institutions have also recognized the value of sourcing new middle-class millionaires from accountants and attorneys: 63.9 percent of them have established a formal value-added or referral program (Exhibit 13.1). These programs are intended to support their financial advisors in creating strategic alliances with lawyers and accountants. What we advocate are strategic partnerships (defined below) as opposed to strategic alliances.

Exhibit 13.1 | Have a Formal Referral Program For Their Financial Advisors

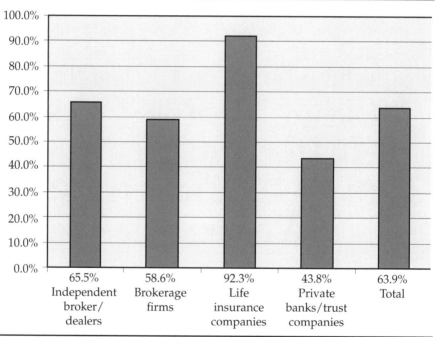

| 65.5% | 58.6% | 92.3% | 43.8% | 63.9% |
| Independent broker/ dealers | Brokerage firms | Life insurance companies | Private banks/trust companies | Total |

N = 108 Financial Institutions
Source: Creating a Pipeline of New Affluent Clients (2003)

In examining the various programs supported by the financial institutions, we have found many of them to be derivative of each other. That is, they advocate the same approaches and provide basically the same tools. The greatest weakness we uncovered is that many of them take a one-size-fits-all approach. This sort of common denominator slant is not enough to provide a financial advisor with the distinctively different approach needed to gain the interest of the accountants and attorneys.

There is no question that a good many financial advisors are indeed garnering new affluent clients from their relationship with accountants and lawyers. Here are four predominant approaches (Exhibit 13.2):

- Financial advisors often contrive reasons to talk to the professional.
- Financial advisors often run from professional to professional promoting the latest hot idea, strategy or product.
- By providing professionals with referrals for their services, financial advisors are looking for "pay back," which they hope is forthcoming.
- In rarer instances, financial advisors create formal joint ventures with professional firms.

Exhibit 13.2 | What Financial Advisors Are Generally Doing Today

Approaches	Actions
Keeping "in front" of the professionals	Social events or lunches
Promoting the new ideas, strategy or product	Innovative products, often tax related
Getting business for the professionals	Hiring referrals directly
Formal joint venture	Firm-to-firm contract, becoming an employee of the professional firm

Source: Creating a Pipeline of New Affluent Clients (2003)

Many financial advisors use a combination of these approaches. And, these various approaches will indeed result in affluent client referrals on an intermittent basis. If this is how you are working today, what we propose is a proven methodology to leverage your current efforts.

First Principals

For the methodology to work effectively you must understand:

- Who the client is
- What a referral "really" is
- The Law of Small Numbers
- The essential role of customization

The client. The accountant or attorney who introduced you to the middle-class millionaire is as much your client as the wealthy individual. While financial advisors, for the most part, express this point of view, very few of them act as if the accountant or attorney is indeed the client. Just as you must work hard to constantly win the loyalty of an affluent client, you must do the same with the accountant or attorney.

A referral defined. In general, a referral from an accountant or attorney is a different animal than a referral from one of your affluent clients. An affluent client referral is best defined as a "hand-off" referral. This is where your wealthy client will direct a middle-class millionaire to you and then step out of the picture. A referral from an accountant or attorney is really a "joint-case work" referral where the affluent client is first and foremost the client of the professional making the referral.

The Law of Small Numbers. We have found that a total of 5 strategic partners—be they accountants or attorneys or other professional advisors—is the ideal number. We did this by constructing a sociometric/revenue potential model. While circumstances can vary when talking about any particular financial advisor, 5 strategic partners is the mathematical point of optimization.

Customization is essential. You will have to tailor your approach to each individual professional.

Understanding and accepting the first principles are critical to success. Consequently, to garner middle-class millionaire clients, you must truly and deeply understand each accountant or attorney you are seeking referrals from. Just as the Whole Client Model is center-stage for providing wealth management to affluent clients, the Professional Profile is center-stage for sourcing new affluent clients from these professionals.

Constructing the *Professional Profile*

In order to make recommendations to wealthy clients, you need to understand what is important to them, what they have, and so forth. The same logic holds true when working with accountants and attorneys.

You start filling out the *professional profile* by noting what you know about a particular accountant or attorney. How do you create this profile? Just ask them. After all, people like to talk about their businesses.

This approach is not much different than what you do when working with an affluent client. In order to develop a detailed profile of the accountant or lawyer you are evaluating as a strategic partner, the following nine areas are often essential:

1. The professionals as people.
2. Their goals and objectives for their practice.
3. Their perspective on various financial services and products.
4. How they are managing their practices.
5. Their current clientele.
6. The marketing approaches they employ.
7. How they are compensated and how this is impacting their lives.
8. Their relationships with financial advisors.
9. Their openness to working with you.

Let's look at each of these areas, including the rationale behind each one as well as sample questions. It is not the specific questions that are important, but the kind of information you need to solicit. The goal is to gain an appreciation of the professional's particular—if not idiosyncratic—world.

The Person. You are looking to determine the professional's history and motivations as well as their evolution in their practices. You are also interested in them as people in order to establish and maintain rapport.

Sample questions:

- How did you get into this business?
- How long have you been at the firm?
- What is your area of expertise?
- Why did you decide to specialize in this area?
- What do you enjoy most about your work?
- What other accounting firms (or law firms) have you been a part of?
- What designations or certifications do you hold?
- Ideally, where would you like to be when you are 45? 55? 65? 75?
- If you did not have to work anymore, what would you do?
- What area of practice were you most interested in during school?
- How long have you and your wife been married?
- How old are your children?
- Are they married, in college, play sports, etc.?
- Do you have grandchildren?
- What do you do to relax?
- What are your hobbies?

Practice goals and objectives. What you are looking for are accountants and attorneys who are motivated to be more financially successful or are seeking to enhance their lifestyles without giving up income. In effect, you are trying to ascertain if the professional you are talking to will respond to the added value you will be providing.

Sample questions:

- How would you describe your role?
- What is your specialty?
- What are the goals and objectives for your practice?
- How important is it to you to build your practice and earn more?
- Where do you see your practice in five years? Ten years?
- How do you see the profits of your practice growing?
- How do you see your client base growing?
- Number of clients?
- Net-worth of clients?
- How important is it to you to work less but maintain your current

income?
- How much free time do you see next year?
- How much pro-bono work do you do?
- How long do you plan on practicing law?
- When do you expect to retire?
- Is there someone at the firm who will eventually succeed you?
- How do you benefit from referring your clients to other professionals in your firm?
- If we were sitting here three years from today, what would have had to happen to make you happy with your practice?

Financial product issues. You need to determine their knowledge and comfort with the financial products you provide. This is most readily seen with respect to life insurance. Say, the lawyer or accountant is not life insurance friendly. That is, they strongly believe in buying term and investing the rest. If you are a financial advisor focusing on selling life insurance, then a professional with this point of view is very unlikely to be a good candidate as a strategic partner.

Sample questions:

- What is the role of life insurance in the planning you do for your clients?
- How do you feel about life insurance as a planning tool?
- Do you feel life insurance is overused or underused in estate planning?
- How familiar are you with the various forms of life insurance and how they can be used?
- What are your thoughts on managed money?
- How much life insurance do you have?
- How do you manage your own money?
- How aware are you of the various state-of-the-art investment strategies?
- When was the last time a client asked you about investments?
- How did you answer it?

Practice management. In order to help your potential strategic partners become more successful you have to understand how they manage their practices today. This covers a very broad range of concerns and factors from their current revenue model to the processes they pursue to work with their wealthy clients. By understanding their practices you will also be able to adapt the way you work with affluent clients into their approach to the matter.

Sample questions:

- How do you build your practice?

- What is the main focus of your practice?
- What percentage of your practice are trusts and estates plans?
- What percentage of your income are trusts and estates plans?
- How do you present ideas and issues to your clients?
- What is your work process?
- What is your follow-up "system"?
- Do you do financial modeling?
- Are you happy with the way your firm works?
- Are you part of a study group?
- How do you allocate profits at your firm?
- How do you illustrate a financial issue or plan to your clients?
- Do you use a computer printout, executive summary, verbally, yellow pad?
- Do your clients usually follow your recommendations?
- How often do you contact your clients either by phone or in person?
- What about your 10 best clients?
- How do you keep current on tax law changes?
- How interested are you in learning about new planning strategies and concepts?
- If estate taxes were repealed, how would this affect your practice?
- What would you do?
- What is the partners/associates ratio?
- What is the staffing breakdown in your practice/firm?
- Do you set practice goals?
- Are you part of the management team?
- How many different practice areas are at your firm?
- How many billable hours are expected of you?
- From your associates?
- What does your typical work week look like?
- How many client meetings do you have per week?
- How many hours per week do you usually put in?
- Would you act as a trustee?

The accountant's or attorney's clientele. In order to leverage the current client base of the accountant or attorney, you have to know what it looks like. We have found that many, if not most financial advisors have an often overly optimistic view of the number and wealth and needs of the clientele of the professionals they are dealing with. What is necessary is to clearly understand the professional's clientele, for this will provide you with an accurate financial assessment of the potential pipeline.

Sample questions:

- How many clients do you have?
- What does having a client entail?

- What markets are you in?
- Do you work with many business owners, executives, retirees, MDs, etc.?
- What does your "typical" client look like?
  - Net-worth.
  - Age.
  - Geographic location.
  - Income.
  - Marital status.
- How did you meet your best client?
- What percentage of your clientele is charitably inclined?
- Describe the values of your typical client.
  - What are examples of things they are doing?
  - Are any of them on the boards of charities?
- How many of your clients are C corporations?
- Do you specialize in any specific industry?
- Do you have a client rating system?
- Do you do automatic reviews?
  - How often?
- What are the average fees per client per year?

Marketing. There is usually a tremendous amount of value you can provide accountants and lawyers when it comes to helping them acquire new wealthy clients. What we have found is that this is one of the strongest forms of economic glue there is. However, in order to add value, you have to first understand what they are doing today, as well as how effective these actions are.

Sample questions:

- How many new clients do you usually get in a year?
- How many new clients do you want to add this year?
- How do you get new clients?
  - Referrals from lawyers, referrals from accountants, referrals from financial advisors, client referrals, seminars, public relations activities, and so forth.
  - (If referrals from another advisor) Where do they get their new clients from?
  - Why do you think this marketing approach works for you?
- Who are your competitors?
- Do you have a marketing director at your firm?
- Do you have a marketing plan?
- Do you use outside marketing advisors?
- What is the image of your firm?
- What are the practice goals for new businesses?
- Membership in local civic, charitable, professional organizations?

- What are your thoughts on multidisciplinary practices?
- What is the firm's viewpoint concerning business development?
- Do you run seminars?
  - What kind?
  - What have been the most successful seminars for you?
  - Do you have seminars for prospects? Advisors?

Compensation. This issue cuts to the essence of the matter of economic glue. The overwhelming percentage of accountants and attorneys are looking for ways to boost their incomes. If you can show them how to modify their compensation arrangements that result in more bottom-line money, you are indeed providing significant value. However, to do so requires that you understand the starting point—where they are today and their point of view on compensation.

Sample questions:

- Do you find that often you are not paid for all the time you put into a case?
- How are profits at your firm determined and allocated?
- How do you generally charge your clients?
  - Hourly rate, fixed fee, success fee.
- How interested are you in other ways of being paid for your expertise that is not based on the hours you put in?
- How has your compensation changed over the last three years?
- Does your firm market any financial products?
- Do you feel your income is commensurate with your efforts?
- Do you have annual client target profits?
- If yes, what are they?
- Do you receive a bonus?
- What is it based on?
- What are the sources of your revenue?
- Has there been any fluctuation in your income of late?
- What do you attribute it to?
- What is the age of your accounts receivable?

Financial Advisors. There is not an accountant or attorney that you want to work with that has not referred their affluent clients to another financial advisor, and probably is doing so today. You need to understand the whole picture when it comes to the professionals you are considering as strategic partners, and their position and experience with financial advisors. This will enable you to place yourself in the best position with an attorney or accountant.

Sample questions:

- How many financial advisors are you currently working with?

- What has been your best and worst experience working with a financial advisor?
- How do you prefer working with a financial advisor?
- Do you have a preference for dealing an with independent's versus a large company's financial advisor?
- How many financial advisors have you shared professional relationships with?
- Do you serve on a Board of Advisors for any financial advisors?
- Do they refer clients to you?
- What is your criterion for the "ideal advisor?"
- Do you have undivided loyalty to any other financial advisors?
  - What is it based on?
- Do you refer business?
- Is there reciprocity?
- What topics/subjects do you seek their expertise?
- What effect have these financial advisors had on your revenue?
- Are you part of a financial advisor's study group?
- How did your clients find their existing financial advisors?
- Who have you worked with in the last 12 months?

Close. The overarching objective is to create a pipeline of new affluent clients by becoming strategic partners with an accountant or attorney. Therefore, you will need to determine if a particular professional is amenable to the idea of working closely with you.

Sample questions:

- Would you be interested in working together to better serve your clients and make your practice more successful?
- How do you feel about someone like me helping you enhance your practice?
- What are the best ways for me to be a resource for you?
- What value do you receive from my process?
  - Financially?
  - Time?
  - Simplicity of life?
- How can I help to make you more money?
- What do I need to do to become your strategic partner?
- Could you see yourself working with me?
- What would it take for you to refer business to me?
- Is there a reason you would not refer me to a client?
- What is the next step?

By conducting the *Professional Profile* you will learn two essential things. One is whether the particular accountant or attorney would make a good strategic partner for you. It is the norm in the financial advisory industry to "sell yourself" to accountants and attorneys. Our perspective—across the board—is that you are a marketer not a sales person. By using the *Professional Profile*, you will find the accountants and attorneys who will enable you to build a very successful practice with middle-class millionaires. Hence, central to this methodology is that you understand you are selecting the accountants and attorneys to partner with; they are not selecting you.

To reiterate, you are the one selecting your strategic partners. You are going to help them to be more successful. Therefore, you are doing the choosing. And all you need to choose is FIVE.

The other essential result of using the *Professional Profile* is that you will be able to identify the economic glue that is crucial to creating the pipeline. Experience using the *Professional Profile* will enable you to readily spot where you can add value to an accountant's or an attorney's practice. The only way you will be able to add value is to know what would be of significant value to a particular attorney or accountant. And, by employing the *Professional Profile* you will uncover their definitions of "value."

Direct and Indirect Financial Incentives

Let's take for granted that you are technically proficient (or can access the appropriate technical expertise by tapping the specialists in your wealth management team), that you are ethical and can play nice with other professionals. These qualities are necessary and are considered givens if you want to generate middle-class millionaire client referrals from accountants and attorneys. However, by themselves, they fall way short of what is required. You will have to move beyond these basics to providing value, which is the "economic glue" that can be used to cement your relationship with accountants and attorneys.

The value is based on financial incentives. There are two types of financial incentives—direct and indirect. While direct financial incentives generate revenue for the accountant or attorney immediately, they are usually impossible for you to consistently provide. On the other hand, indirect financial incentives are not limited in the same way, and they can be instrumental in enabling you to meaningfully differentiate yourself.

There are a number of commonly employed direct financial incentives including:

- *Reciprocal referrals.* The problem is the near impossibility that you can really trade referrals with the accountants and attorneys you know. While you will certainly provide referrals to accountants and attorneys when the opportunities arise, you do not want to be dependent on giving a wealthy client referral in order to receive a wealthy client referral.

- *Sharing in the revenues from financial product sales.* For those attorneys or accountants who are properly set up and licensed to share in the revenues from financial product sales, you should certainly pursue it. However, we repeatedly find that less than five percent of attorneys and no more than 20 percent of accountants are interested in this from of compensation. If you only approached generating professional referrals in this way, you would be ignoring the vast majority of potential professional referral sources.

- *Generating significant professional fees.* Here, you would hire the accountant or attorney to do tax or legal work for you. There are certain ethical considerations that need to be taken into account, such as your need for the tax or legal work. These ethical considerations tend to derail this form of direct financial incentives.

With direct financial incentives not being the answer, we need to turn to indirect financial incentives. They are another form of "economic glue." With indirect financial incentives, you are providing practice-building support to the accountant or attorney.

Two critical areas where you can provide indirect financial incentives for the accountants and attorneys are:

- *Practice management.* Your ability to share best practices in cultivating middle-class millionaires, for example, is likely to be in high demand from accountants and attorneys. The research-based insights (see **Part I: The Middle-Class Millionaire**) is a very good example of the type of knowledge accountants and attorneys are interested in, and the type of information you can provide that will translate into affluent client referrals from these professionals. Another example would be the methodology for creating loyal affluent clients (see *Chapter 5: The "6C" Framework for Creating Loyal Affluent Clients*).

- *Marketing support and ideas.* What we are talking about here are ways for attorneys and accountants to get more wealthy clients without depending on referrals from the financial advisors. For example, there is the opportunity to provide some of them with superior client assessment and management methodologies and tools. We have found that it is the norm for accountants and attorneys not to have a holistic understanding of their affluent clients and this results in limiting the business they do with these wealthy clients. Therefore, sharing the Whole Client Model has been instrumental in garnering affluent client referrals for a large number of financial advisors. Along the same lines, educating the professionals on the nine high-net-worth personalities has also proven very effective (see *Chapter 6: Positioning Yourself Using High-Net-Worth Psychology*).

The ability to identify the appropriate indirect financial incentives is predicated on your ability to meaningfully profile the individual accountant or attorney. Consequently, the *Professional Profile* is necessary.

Expanding Your Strategic Partnerships

Once you have established a strategic partnership with an accountant or attorney, you will need to expand the relationship. In effect, with the pipeline built for you to receive a steady stream of new middle-class millionaire client referrals, it is still necessary to make sure more and more wealthy clients are being put into the pipeline.

You will need to continue to communicate that you are competent and ethical. You will need to also be delivering value in the form of indirect financial incentives. However, to make sure you are receiving as many affluent client referrals as possible requires you to help your strategic partners to think more expansively about their wealthy clients and where you can fit in.

More often than not, accountants and attorneys will only consider affluent clients they are currently dealing with. You need them to think about affluent clients who they are not presently providing services to.

You also need your strategic partners to be proactive in looking for middle-class millionaires that they can refer to you. While these professionals will often (not always) respond to inquiries for financial advisors from their wealthy clients, you need for them to be actively investigating opportunities to bring you in on.

Part of the methodology that creates a pipeline of affluent clients from accountants and attorneys is making certain there is a steady stream of new wealthy individuals for you to work with. There are a number of potential components to this phase. Three of the more effective components are:

- *Identifying and constantly adding value.* It is a mistake to assume that once you have identified the value the accountant or attorney is interested in, and you deliver those indirect financial incentives, that you are home free. For your strategic partners, what is "value" will constantly evolve. Therefore, you need to constantly update their *Professional Profiles* and adjust accordingly.

- *Presenting targeted state-of-the-art strategies and financial products.* Many accountants and attorneys are not familiar with the various state-of-the-art strategies and financial products, giving you the opportunity to supply the education. Broadly speaking, what you are looking to do is introduce and explain a strategy or product that will prompt the professional to think of a wealthy client for whom the strategy or product will be appropriate.

- *Conducting strategic scenario sessions.* This is an especially effective way of identifying affluent referral opportunities. Here, you work with the accountant or attorney (sometimes with the assistance of a facilitator) to discuss their existing wealthy clientele, as well as the affluent people they are prospecting. In these sessions, a game plan is constructed for each qualified client or prospect. We have found that using the Whole Client Model as the framework to discuss their affluent clients and prospects is especially effective. *Strategic scenario sessions* are the very best ways to ensure that the pipeline is full.

Practice Implications

As we have seen, it is critical that you actively and methodically garner middle-class millionaire client referrals from accountants and attorneys (see *Chapter 11: Focus on Referrals*). However, to accomplish this agenda requires most financial advisors to think and act differently than they are used to.

There is a proven and powerful methodology for creating a pipeline of new middle-class millionaires from accountants and referrals. This methodology starts with what we call first principles, which means acting as if the professional making the affluent client referral is the "client," understanding that when they make referrals they remain part of the team, that you need no more than five accountants and/or attorneys to become incredibly successful and you will need to customize your approach, as well as your way of doing business for each of these five.

Becoming adept with the *Professional Profile* is next on the list. You cannot deliver value to an accountant or attorney unless you know how they define value. Moreover, you must know if it is worth your time and effort to work with a particular accountant or attorney. The *Professional Profile* is a tool that leverages your skills and expertise in fact finding with affluent clients and applies them to a different audience.

By employing the *Professional Profile*, you will discover how to add value to a particular accountant's or attorney's practice. Indirect financial incentives in the form of practice management and marketing support are usually the best ways for you to add value to your strategic partners.

Finally, to keep the pipeline full, you need to always be on the lookout for ways to add value. Additionally, educating your strategic partners on targeted state-of-the-art financial strategies and products is advised. Optimally, conducting *strategic scenario sessions* with them results in a steady stream of new wealthy clients for you to see.

So, in conclusion:

- *What kind of indirect financial incentives are you most comfortable with?*

- *If asked, how would you describe a strategic scenario session to one of your strategic partners?*

Exercise #1 | Creating Your *Professional Profile* Question List

1. Take each of the sample questions we provided and rate them 1 (right for me), 2 (maybe appropriate) and 3 (not right for me).
2. Take all the questions you rated #1 and jot down how they will help you develop a deep understanding of an accountant or an attorney.
3. Identify 3 questions—rated 1—from each category that you feel are essential for you to have answered.

You cannot possibly ask all the sample questions we provided. When coaching financial advisors on this methodology, we have found they want to know which questions are most important to ask. We have found that different financial advisors end up determining different questions to be "most important." This is a function of their individual personalities and styles. So, this exercise will help you determine which questions are likely to be "most important" for you to ask.

Exercise #2 | Sharing the Knowledge

1. Identify the marketing strategies and processes you use to source middle-class millionaire clients.
2. Identify the practice management methodologies and processes you employ to make your financial advisory practice run more effectively.
3. On a scale of 1 (not at all applicable) to 10 (extremely applicable), rate each of the marketing and practice management "ideas" you cited based on how well they might work for an accountant or attorney.
4. How would you introduce those market and practice management "ideas" you rated 8, 9 or 10 to one of your strategic partners?

We have found that most financial advisors have a plethora of marketing and practice management tools and techniques, methodologies and tactics that can be readily used—sometimes with minor modifications—by accountants and attorneys who are similarly looking to build their practices with affluent clients. By taking the time to specify what these are, you are in a better position to quickly provide indirect financial incentives.

KEY LESSONS

There are all sorts of ways to source middle-class millionaire clients. However, by far, the most effective approach is through referrals. First of all, referrals from your other clients are something you should be ardently pursuing. Moreover, referrals from "centers of influence"—accountants and attorneys—can be an even more productive prospecting approach.

Most financial advisors are not doing a very good job of garnering affluent client referrals from their own clients. They, on the whole, are even more ineffective when it comes to garnering middle-class millionaire client referrals from "centers of influence."

At its core, the problem for most financial advisors is not knowing how to solicit affluent client referrals from these sources. The financial advisors are not adept at, nor do they have a process for, obtaining these referrals.

This problem is corrected with the seven-step affluent client referral methodology and the pipeline methodology. Both these processes are highly systematic, completely repeatable and have been proven to work extremely well in the real world.

Both methodologies leverage your skills and expertise. They are new only to the extent they are forcing you to apply your abilities in different ways. With these methodologies there is no paradigm shift of thinking out of the box. That is what makes them so effective. They are predicated on doing what you can do well; just doing these things in a slightly different environment or for a different audience.

The seven-step affluent client referral methodology centers on loyal wealthy clients, the Whole Client Model and asking. All these skills and processes you need to be adept at anyway, irrespective of you getting new affluent client referrals from your current clients, so why not get the referrals.

Regarding obtaining a steady stream of middle-class millionaire referrals from "centers of influence," we're talking about fact-finding using the *Professional Profile,* and then using what you have learned to identify, and subsequently provide, indirect financial incentives. Experience shows us that many of the indirect financial incentives are the insights, methodologies, tools and tactics you employ to cultivate middle-class millionaires.

While we are not dealing with a sea change, you will nevertheless need to become proficient with some new approaches and tools. As with learning any new skill, success follows practice.

MOVING UP-MARKET

- *Are you interested in working with clients who are wealthier than middle-class millionaires?*
- *Do the ultra-affluent appeal to you as clients?*
- *With respect to the methodologies, tools and tactics we have detailed here, what applicability do they have to wealthier clients, such as the ultra-affluent?*
- *What are the limitations of the methodologies, tools and tactics?*

As we have seen, middle-class millionaires—those with liquid assets ranging from $500,000 to $5 million—are the "ideal clients" for a preponderance of financial advisors as well as financial institutions (see *Chapter 1: Who Is The Middle-Class Millionaire*). Based on a clientele of these "ideal clients," you should be able to create a successful financial advisory practice that translates into quite a nice living.

While being able to cultivate middle-class millionaire clients can make you very successful as a financial advisor, we have found that there are some advisors who want to move up-market even more: They want to cultivate clients with more than $5 million in investable assets. They want to find and work with clients whose net-worth exceeds $10 million. Indeed, every financial advisor would agree: the more money the wealthy client has the better.

So, in conclusion, we will briefly address how the methodologies, tools and tactics you need to master to cultivate middle-class millionaire clients are also essential if you choose to move up-market. And, fortunately, the skills you need to go up-market—$10 million and above—are similar to the skills necessary to cultivate middle-class millionaire clients.

Client Loyalty Is Still Client Loyalty

Whether the affluent client has $500,000 or $5 million or $50 million in investable assets, you want that client to be loyal. Client loyalty, irrespective of wealth, will translate into a much more profitable financial advisory firm.

We have found that the "6C" Framework that is critical to creating loyal middle-class millionaire clients is just as critical to creating exceptionally wealthy loyal clients as well. One of the biggest differences is that the exceptionally wealthy are more value/cost sensitive than middle-class millionaires because so many financial advisors seek to serve them. This means that you have to be especially adept at communicating your value.

Another significant difference is the increasing importance of being consultative. The exceptionally wealthy are much more likely than middle-class millionaires to be displeased by financial advisors who promote any type of financial product. It's a prerequisite that you be highly consultative.

In moving up-market, your ability to create loyal affluent clients takes on ever-greater importance. Much more time and effort will usually have to be devoted to building intense professional relationships with the exceptionally wealthy. The good news, however, is that the methodology for doing so is the very same methodology you need to master to create loyal middle-class millionaire clients.

Family Office Services—Wealth Management Writ Large

As we have seen, wealth management is the optimal practice model for working with middle-class millionaires. To a large degree, it is the same practice model desired by wealthier clients. When you get to families of significant wealth, wealth management takes on new dimensions and is known as family office services.

In the world of family offices, financial advisors are providing a variety of financial products and services. Aside from investment management, family offices deliver administrative services, such as bill paying. Many also oversee the delivery of advanced planning services, such as wealth transfer and asset protection services. And, family offices, to meet the needs of their exceptionally wealthy clientele, often provide a full complement of lifestyle services, such as personal security services and medical advocacy services.

What makes the delivery of family office services work is the very same methodology, tools and tactics that makes the delivery of wealth management work. The Whole Client Model is even more important when the level of wealth increases. The need to dig deep and be able to identify all the inter-relationships as well as uncover opportunities makes using the Whole Client Model so essential.

Family offices are usually outsourced operations. Most of the family offices use outside vendors to deliver their services—with the management of the family office overseeing everything. The family offices are looking to bring in the appropriate specialists when they have a need. This is the exact same model as wealth management with just a larger menu of services and products.

The Increasing Importance of Professional Advisor Referrals

As you look to go up-market, your ability to garner referrals to the exceptionally wealthy from even loyal clients is mitigated. Save for stellar investment performance, the very wealthy are not inclined to make referrals to their very wealthy peers. While there are exceptions (which means you should pursue exceptionally wealthy client referrals whenever possible), the more efficacious route to the exceptionally wealthy is by cultivating "centers of influence."

Accountants and attorneys take on added importance. Because their personal and business lives are all the more complex, the exceptionally wealthy tend to rely more heavily on these professionals. This translates into their accountants and attorneys having even more influence regarding the financial advisors the exceptionally wealthy choose to employ.

The same methodology for garnering middle class millionaire clients from accountants and attorneys is applicable to sourcing the exceptionally wealthy. What we often see is that financial advisors who master this methodology are first referred to middle-class millionaires and if they do well by them are often referred to the handful of exceptionally wealthy clients the professional works with.

Practice Implications

If your objective is to move up-market—or at a minimum add a few exceptionally wealthy clients to your practice—then the good news is the same methodologies, tools and tactics you can use to cultivate middle-class millionaires just as appropriate. Adjustments are usually required, but the underlying processes and mechanisms are the same. By mastering the "how to" elements in this book you will be able to apply them to cultivating the exceptionally wealthy as you build a highly successful financial advisory practice with middle-class millionaires.

Appendix

THE SEVEN GUIDELINES FOR SELECTING A COACH

- *How would you define phenomenal success?*
- *What are you going to do that's going to enable you to achieve your goal of phenomenal success?*
- *Is there a gap between your current income and the income you want to earn?*
- *Are you working with clients who possess the level of wealth that will permit you to reach your financial objective?*

———————

Coaching is becoming more pervasive throughout the financial advisory industry. Financial advisors are increasingly turning to a variety of different types of coaches, from peer and wholesalers to field management and professional coaches in order to enable them to achieve greater success.

Extensive empirical research has shown that coaching can indeed result in greater success. But, it is critical for you to understand what coaching is about and then to carefully select a coach, examining the coach's credentials and teaching philosophy.

Coaching For Success

Our coaching process is focused on the bottom line. That is, we focus on generating significant increases in income. For us:

Coaching for success is a process of education, focus and accountability **that enhances the economic achievement of financial advisors.**

This definition is "what we truly want to accomplish through coaching," which is to facilitate the *economic achievement* of financial advisors. By economic achievement or success, we are talking about *income*. As coaches, the way we do this is through a focused educational process, which is multifaceted, often intricate and requires accountability from the financial advisor.

By approaching coaching in this manner, a very essential benefit emerges: *Clients are better served*. Often financial advisors choose to hire a coach in order to do a better job for their clients. This is laudable. However, when an *ethical financial advisor* through the services of a coach achieves a greater level of financial success, that financial success comes about because his or her clients have been better served.

Coaching in not only about clients, it is about you. We believe that over a year, if you are intensively using a coach's services during that time, you should see your income go up by **25 percent or more**. In effect, your income after all expenses including the cost of the coaching should, at a minimum, rise by 25 percent in a year's time.

Guidelines for Selecting a Coach

In Exhibit A.1, we provide you with the seven guidelines we recommend you follow in choosing a particular coach to work with.

Exhibit A.1 | Guidelines for Selecting a Coach

Guidelines	Example Questions
1: Your self-assessment	• In what areas do you need help? • If you received help in these areas, how will it affect your economic success?
2: The coach's philosophical orientation	• How does the coach define success? • Who does the coach tend to take on as clients?
3: The coach's process	• What are the responsibilities of all parties? • What is the coach's pedagogical approach?

Exhibit A.1 | Guidelines for Selecting a Coach (continued)

4: The coach's areas of expertise	• What specialized knowledge and skills does the coach possess? • What is the basis of their specialized knowledge and skills?
5: The coach's background	• What makes the coach qualified to be a coach? • What is the coach's experience and "track record" at coaching?
6: The coach's business model	• How is the coach compensated? • How does the coach manage his or her operation?
7: The projected economic success you should expect	• What is your projected financial return for employing the coach? • What is the time frame you are looking at to achieve this financial return?

Source: Selecting a Coach (2005)

Let's now consider each of the guidelines in greater detail:

- *Guideline 1: Your self-assessment.* To begin with, you have to decide whether you believe that a coach, of one stripe or another, can be of service to you.
- *Guideline 2: The coach's philosophical orientation.* Your coach must be able meet your needs and wants as they relate to your financial advisory practice. Therefore, it is essential that you understand the philosophical orientation of your prospective coach and agree with it. You'll also divine a coach's philosophical orientation by who he or she accepts as clients. How selective is the coach, and why? By knowing the coach's clients you are able to get a good grasp of what they are about.
- *Guideline 3: The coach's process.* What you need to understand is how the coach works, his or her "process." Very importantly, what are his or her responsibilities and what are yours? By having a clear understanding of your end of the bargain and what you are committing to, you maximize the success of your coaching experience. Another aspect of the coach's process you need to be aware of is his or her teaching approach.
- *Guideline 4: The coach's areas of expertise.* Consider coaching with a specific set of objectives in mind. This way you can ask: "So, what makes this coach qualified to help me with my objectives?" You need to know the coach's specialized knowledge and skill sets. Furthermore,

you need to know the basis of this expertise.

- *Guideline 5: The coach's background.* This guideline is often closely aligned with the coach's areas of expertise. You need to know what qualifies the coach to be a coach and some part of his or her personal history. For example, what are their credentials—formal and informal—that makes them a coach?

- *Guideline 6: The coach's business model.* You will also want to know something about the business model of the coach. Clearly, you need to know how he or she is compensated. The way people make their money is one of the very best indicators of their current and future behaviors. You should also learn something about the coach's operation. By having a good idea of what you are looking for from the coach, as well as a basic idea of his or her infrastructure, you can decide if it works for you.

- *Guideline 7: The projected economic success you should expect.* The coach is there to help you improve your business. Therefore, you should have a pretty good idea of the income increases you should expect from working with a coach. You should also recognize that if you choose to use the services of a high-quality coach on an on-going basis, you should realistically anticipate a *25 percent annual income increase or better* in the first year, provided that you put in the requisite time and effort.

Practice Implications

If you are like most financial advisors, coaching may be the best way for you to fast-track to a higher level of financial success. Be careful: There are many people calling themselves coaches these days; many of them are not qualified. You must take care when selecting a coach. There are seven guidelines that you should use when deciding on which coach is right for you. Although they interconnect in many ways, it is important that you are able to obtain a coach's answers to the questions these guidelines pose.

THE AUTHORS

RUSS ALAN PRINCE

Russ Alan Prince is president of the market research and consulting firm Prince & Associates Inc., and he is a leading authority on the private wealth industry. Mr. Prince consults to high-net-worth families on accessing various family office and wealth management services. He also works with financial and legal experts who provide cutting-edge strategies and concepts to families with exceptional wealth. Mr. Prince is a columnist with various publications and is the author of 31 books.

DAVID A. GERACIOTI

David Geracioti is editor of *Registered Rep.*, the leading magazine for investment professionals.

Books authored and co-authored by Russ Alan Prince
1. *Selecting a Coach: Seven Guidelines For Financial Advisors* (CFPN, 2005).
2. *Inside The Family Office: Managing the Fortunes of The Exceptionally Wealthy* (Wealth Management Press, 2004).
3. *Safe & Sound: A Proven Methodology For Protecting The Wealthy* (National Underwriter, 2004).
4. *Women of Wealth: Understanding Today's Affluent Female Investor* (National Underwriter, 2004).
5. *The Private Client Lawyer: Now And in The Future* (Wealth Management Press, 2003).
6. *Creating a Pipeline of New Affluent Clients: Building Strategic Partnerships With Lawyers & Accountants* (National Underwriter, 2003).
7. *Wealth Management: The New Business Model For Financial Advisors* (Wealth Management Press, 2003).
8. *Accountants as Wealth Managers: The New Paradigm For Providing Financial Services* (Institutional Investor, 2003).
9. *Advanced Planning With The Ultra-Affluent: A Framework For Professional Advisors* (Institutional Investor, 2002).

10. *Giving Wisely: Maximizing Your Charitable Giving* (Giving Capital, 2002).
11. *The World of Registered Representatives: Insights And Opportunities For Brokerage And Investment Management Firms* (Institutional Investor, 2002).
12. *The Millionaire's Advisor: High-Touch, High-Profit Relationship Management Strategies of Advisors to The Wealthy* (Institutional Investor, 2002).
13. *eWealth: Understanding The Internet Millionaire* (Institutional Investor, 2001).
14. *Marketing Mutual Funds Through Independent Advisors* (Institutional Investor, 2001).
15. *Value-Added Wholesaling: The New Paradigm For Marketing Financial Products Through Advisors* (Institutional Investor, 2000).
16. *Advisor 2000: Strategies For Success in The New Millennium* (High-Net-Worth Press, 2000).
17. *High-Net-Worth Psychology: Finding, Winning and Keeping Affluent Investors* (High-Net-Worth Press, 1999).
18. *Winning The War For The Wealthy: How Life Insurance Companies Can Dominate The Upscale Markets* (High-Net-Worth Press, 1999).
19. *Private Wealth: Insights in The High-Net-Worth Market* (Institutional Investor, 1999).
20. *The Perfect Legacy: How to Establish Your Own Private Foundation* (High-Net-Worth Press, 1998).
21. *The Charitable Giving Handbook* (National Underwriter, 1997).
22. *Cultivating The Affluent II: Leveraging High-Net-Worth Client And Advisor Relationships* (Institutional Investor, 1997).
23. *Building Your Business: Marketing Your Way to a $100 Million Investment Advisory Practice* (High-Net-Worth Press, 1997).
24. *Physician Financial Planning in a Changing Environment* (McGraw Hill, 1996).
25. *Marketing Through Advisors: A Toolkit For Life Insurance Professionals* (National Underwriter, 1996).
26. *Marketing to Family Business Owners: A Toolkit For Life Insurance Professionals* (National Underwriter, 1996).
27. *Building an Affluent Clientele: Marketing Personal Lines to The Wealthy* (National Underwriter, 1996).
28. *Cultivating the Affluent: How to Segment and Service the High-Net-Worth Market* (Institutional Investor, 1995).
29. *Marketing to the Affluent: A Toolkit For Life Insurance Professionals* (National Underwriter, 1995).
30. *The Charitable Estate Planning Process: How to Find And Work With The Philanthropic Affluent* (Lexington House, 1994).
31. *The Seven Faces of Philanthropy: A New Approach to Cultivating Major Donors* (Wiley, 1994).